The Prairie Spy:

Who Shot the Dryer?

And Other Stories

From the Home Front

To the World Tribe of Girls,
and especially to my own.

The Prairie Spy:

Who Shot the Dryer?

And Other Stories

From the Home Front

By
Alan "Lindy" Linda

Trellis Publishing, Inc.
P.O. Box 280
New York Mills, MN 56567
800-513-0115

www.trellispublishing.com

The Prairie Spy: Who Shot the Dryer? And Other Stories From the Home Front

Publisher's Cataloging-in-Publication
(Provided by Quality Books, Inc.)

Linda, Alan "Lindy".
    The prairie spy : who shot the dryer? : and other
  stories from the home front / by Alan "Lindy" Linda
    p. cm.
    ISBN 978-1-930650-40-4

    1.. City and town life--Humor. 2. Soldiers--Vietnam--
Fiction. 3. Short stories, American.   I. Title.

PS3612.I546P73 2012   813'.6
                    QBI12-600048

10 9 8 7 6 5 4 3 2 1

Cover and Interior Design by Design Angler, Inc.

Table of Contents

The Prairie Spy

Introduction

Once, a long time ago in a writing class, the instructor said to me, in an effort to convince me that journalism was an honorable undertaking, "What are you going to write about? You cannot just write writing!" Meaning, of course, that my life wasn't as interesting as anyone else's.

The sure cure for that is to live longer than everyone else. That's my goal at the moment, because a lot of the content of the last twenty years of columns has been about other people.

Oh, sure, there's a lot of autobiographical stuff in there, too, like growing up on a farm, being the last to graduate from the country school system in Iowa, being drafted out of college into the Army and sent to Vietnam, then trying to leave the USA and getting only as far as New York Mills on the way to Canada (A rather confused attempt at fleeing after Vietnam, rather than before.), farming a little, going into business for myself, being raised by My Tribe of Girls (One Old Girl; three Young Girls), buying a hardware store, learning to fly, and always, like a golden thread through all the silver lining, playing in weekend rock and roll bands.

Twenty-some years of weekly column writing is the diamond that reflects the shine from the silver and gold, sort of. This book contains parts and pieces of that diamond, the three biggest ones being my three daughters, The Young Girls.

Now, appliances: I first began to sense that appliances could communicate with me when, three days out of Vietnam, abruptly enrolled at Iowa State University, in the basement of the only place which I could find to live on such short notice, the large fat-boy furnace with the huge, round arms seemed able to protect me from the refrigerator, which I had concluded in a post-traumatic bout with reality, was trying to poison me. It was years later, after some years of striving to master repairing these appliances, that they first began to actually speak to me.

Of course, I had taken at that point several years of arduous training in communication with The Tribe of Girls, and had learned the hard way from them how to communicate wordlessly by subtle facial changes, minute shoulder movements, barely discernible posture adjustments, and once in a great while, impossible anatomical requests suggested by one or more human fingers. Appliances talking to me? Nothing after that. A thousand words in a glance from A Girl was more than adequate training for a few pages of a technical manual or a squeak and a rattle from a dryer or a furnace.

Words continue to be a wonder to me, have in fact been so ever since I can remember. I hope those here are as wonderful for you.

I specially thank My True Love, MaryBee, mostly for being in my life and gratefully for helping publish this book.

The Prairie Spy

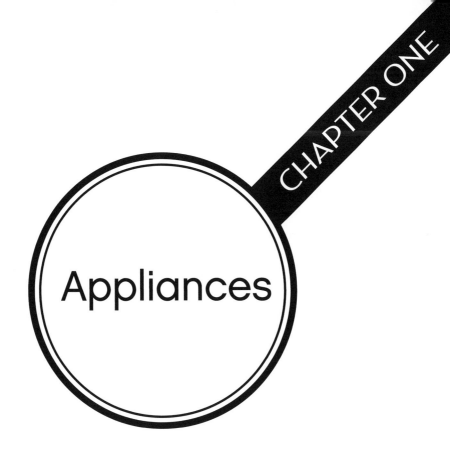

Appliances

Who Shot Ms. Frigidaire the Dryer?

For those of you out there who are new readers, and have wondered which drugs I'm on currently, here comes more reason for concern.

As you know, I made a large part of my livelihood servicing home appliances, and there came a day, after puzzling over what was wrong with various washing machines, dryers, water heaters, furnaces, and so forth for many years, I realized that they were communicating with me.

I was surprised, let me tell you. There I was in a farm house, answering a call from the woman of the house that went like this: "I heard gun shots from the electric dryer! Can you come out right away, please? I'm afraid to even open the dryer door."

Gun shots? Let me tell you something else: I answered the phone every day hoping and praying that someone would call and report the OK Corral in their electric dryer. I moved her to the top of the list, strapped on my tool holster, saddled up the service truck, and raced out there.

I plugged in a trouble light, and, holding the light before me as somewhat of a shield in case someone inside there was still alive and had bullets left, eased the door open with my lucky pliers. (I'm not into witchcraft or magic, but I won't go anywhere without my lucky pliers.)

Such a tragedy I have never witnessed. Nor such a surprise, because it was then that Ms. Frigidaire The Dryer, of a family known for its cool repose in a clothing crisis, began to talk. "Gasp," she said, "I've been shot." Then silence while I opened the door further.

Who's in there, I said, while for the first time wondering what was in that vitamin pill I had taken that morning. Then I thought back further. Maybe I shouldn't have inhaled back in the sixties. I thought that I had heard a voi......

"Please help me," said a feminine voice.

Who are you, I asked?

"Don't go stupid on me now," said the she voice, "I've heard on the clothes line that you're quite intelligent, and I'm dying from several gunshot wounds, so get on with it."

Ummmm, let's see, what were those three rules from the Red Cross first aid course. Three "A"s, I think. Or was it ABC. That would be air way for one, so I quickly raced outside and checked the dryer's vent for restriction, and found a huge glob of wool fibers. I'd have to talk to these people about running wool rugs through their d......

"Quit day dreaming," said Ms. Frigidaire, "and get back in here." She sounded a bit more breathy, now that she could breathe again. She also sounded bossier. The second A, the second B. Look, I told her, I'm having a little trouble remembering my triage triangle, so…

Ms. Frigidaire said: "Good grief! See all the holes in my drum lung? You have to plug them up or I'll, I'll…" I'll what. Get more bossy?

It was then that I found out what had happened. Someone, probably one of the teenage sons, had left several rounds of ammunition in his pants pocket and when they made it to the heat of the electric dryer, they had corked off. Ms. Frigidaire had several slugs embedded in her. I whistled in admiration of the privilege of getting to do this kind of surgery, and grabbed my lucky pliers.

"Ouch," she said, as I wriggled at the first lead slug and worked it out of her. "Are you a medical doctor or a veterinarian?"

Are you in pain, I asked her, because I can unplug you and put you under while I check out the rest of you.

"Don't you dare," she snorted. "I know your type. While I'm under, you'll look under my up-top and at my down-there and who knows what."

I yanked the next bullet out quite rudely. She grunted. I dropped this one from my pliers into a small magnetic dish I used. It went clank when it hit. I began to feel like Hawkeye on MASH.

This next one, I told her? It's quite close to your temperature control?

"Yes," she replied, "so what?" Boy. She swallows a bunch of bullets, which was her own fault, and goes all bitchy. Women! I'd show her.

Well, I said, the temperature control is close to your small framus, which itself lies upon your encabulator, which connects a secondary incandescent tubulus to the primary revolvaling. The revolvaling, I was going to say, looks like it's had some hard wear on its rotalingual nervapling, but she interrupted me.

"Am I going to make it," she meekly asked me.

Well, I said as I removed the last bullet, you've got more holes in you than a spaghetti strainer, but I think you'll be ok.

I finished up and left her with a bottle of perfume—she wasn't all that fresh, Frigidaire, that's French, right? They don't bathe so much, I think.

I'd be back, I told her, to give her a complete physical next month.

She slammed her lid shut and closed her service door.

"Not in this life," she hissed.

Back when I couldn't hear appliances talk, life was simpler.

§

Dave Lennox the Furnace

"I'm all stuffed up," said the nasally voice of The Dave Lennox Series 3 oil furnace to me. "I can't breathe." When he said "breathe," it sounded like "breed." He was really plugged up.

I was out on a call, in an advisory role to some young folks who had just purchased a house. They wanted to know what was wrong, why the house wouldn't heat, why it was costing an arm and a leg for fuel oil.

Truth to say, it's fun to prowl around strange appliances, talk to the furnaces, and figure out how to make the whole HVAC (heating, ventilating, air conditioning) scenario work better. Figuring out furnaces is similar to the way doctors figure out people. Take some pressures, take some temperatures, give the customer the results and say: "We need to run some more tests."

You run more tests: you practice your craft on the customer: you wait to see if they, or, in my case, it, gets better. Sometimes it does. Sometimes it doesn't. Then you charge them several hundred bucks and hope you got it right.

"Am I dying?" asked The Dave Lennox Series 3, as I felt his forehead (hot air plenum) to see what his temperature was. I tried to keep my face from showing my alarm, either to Mr. Series 3, or to the customers, the young man and woman who were standing by, as concerned about their furnace as any new mother or father might be about their child.

In fact, he was burning up. And he was swelled up. His upper respiratory tract (hot air plenum to the layman) was bulged out with his attempts to breathe, and every time he came on, his lungs went "Bong!" And when he shut off, the same thing, "Bong!"

How long have you felt like this, I asked him.

"Well," he replied, his throat husky with the effort, "ever since those idiot home owners ran out of money and decided they could hook me up themselves."

When was that, I asked him, while I was palpating his esophageal passage. (Return air duct, what he inhaled through. A good air circulation system for a furnace is much more complex than the human throat, which inhales and exhales through just one simple passage. Furnace air systems can be restricted on either end.)

He said, "About 12 years ago." And then he gasped, and the fire in him died. Suddenly, he was unconscious, although his lungs continued to attempt to force air through his restricted passageways.

I glanced over at the home owners, who hadn't realized what they were seeing, which was good. Well, good for them. The Dave Lennox Series 3 was in extreme distress, and here I was without my medical tools.

I pulled his front cover, lifted the lifeless metal lid on his fan-limit control, and checked the amount of bimetal rotation on the temperature dial. Sure enough, it was hard over on the high temp side. He was going out on me.

Dave! Dave! Can you hear me? Don't quit on me, you hear me? You're tough enough to put up with this for 12 years, just hang on a few more minutes.

What was happening was attributable to the original owner-installers, who naively believed that a few pieces of trunk duct, a couple of round supply pipes, and hey! We're done here. What that produced was a severe air restriction on both sides of the equation. Dave couldn't get enough air to breathe, which didn't much matter, because even if he had, he wouldn't have been able to get rid of it anyway. Heat prostration, brought on by hypoxia.

To be honest, there was a moment there when I thought about simply letting him go. He'd had a rough life. He was about 65 in human years.
But then I realized I was about that old myself.
I turned to the young owners, and with enough urgency to carry the importance of my request, asked for a hammer and a screwdriver. I said, "Quick! He's out cold."
What I had to do was an emergency tracheotomy, open a hole in his throat so he could breathe. I took the screwdriver, momentarily hesitated as I searched for just the right spot, and used the hammer to pound the screwdriver sideways through the sheet metal. I opened a large flap there, which I pried open.
I was a bit surprised. He came back immediately. These Dave Lennox Series 3's are tough customers.
"Thanks," Dave said, in a nice clear voice. "I've been fainting several times a day for 12 years. I just didn't realize how bad it was."
I gave the owners a list of actions that were needed to permanently improve the situation, and hit the road.

§

Murray the Mower

"That gasoline you're pouring into me looks funny," said Murray the Mower to me yesterday, as I was filling his tank. It was time for the first mowing. Murray the Mower was tired of sitting in the corner of the shed all winter. Going for a drive excited him. All guy, that Murray.

"What do you mean, it looks funny?"

"It looks like water. Look at it. Are you sure that's gas? I've never seen gas that water clear before?" I looked at it. It did look pretty clear. None of that usual darkness of color to it. I smelled it.

"It doesn't have much of a smell," I told Murray the Mower.

"Then don't dump that stuff in," he said. "Better test it. You know if the new ethanol gas sits around very long it will attract its weight in water," Murray the Mower said. All guy. He likes to go fast. No watered down gas for him.

"Ah! That's just a myth. I've had this can plugged up tight." I've heard this one before, and I've had my share of trouble with water in stored gas, but usually, it's been my fault. But it did look funny.

"Maybe you should go ask General Electric the Washing Machine," Murray the M. said to me. General Electric is in charge of all household appliances. Like all good generals, it appears he has been spreading his command outward.

"Have you been talking to The General?" I asked Murray the Mower. Lately, The General has been all bent out of shape because The Speed Queen, my dryer, has been blaming him for her inability to quickly and efficiently dry clothes. She says he's been forwarding damp laundry to her. She whispered to me one evening, in a stage voice that you could have heard one township over: "I don't think he's got any zing in his spin. Maybe you should get him some Laundry Viagra."

That pretty much upset General Electric, who won't put up with much hint of anything less than total respect from his troops. Like all good soldiers everywhere, if you rat out The General, you're damned if you do, and damned if you don't. Say The General tells you to tie some pants into knots, or to pose them in sexually lewd positions, or to try to torture information out of them, you'd better do it. At that moment, the Geneva Convention is far, far away, and The General is very, very close. Do what he says, and The Convention might punish you. Don't do it, and The General certainly will. It's an old story, but people still think soldiers can perform their jobs any old way they choose. Yeah, right.

So anyway, I went to ask General Electric if he thought this gasoline might not be up to snuff. "Pour some into me," he said.

"Listen," I said to him, "I came down here for an opinion, not for you to sniff and get high."

"Pour it in," he repeated. "I'll just sample it and spin it down the drain."

About then, Lady Kenmore the Electric Dryer piped up and said, "Oh good grief! Now I'm going to get laundry that'll set me on fire."

General Electric promptly retorted: "No one has been able to set your pants on fire in over twenty years, get a life!"

Lady Kenmore replied: "They haven't been heated up since you decided you're a woman living in a man's body."

"Wait!" I said to them both. "Will you two please settle down. Just because The General has decided he might be gay doesn't mean he isn't human. He deserves some respect." I think it's old battlefield stress confusing him. I turned to the dryer: "And just because you're nearly into dryer menopause doesn't mean you aren't still attractive."

I thought for a moment and added: "If you guys don't start getting along, I'm going to unplug you both."

They both harrumphed, but remained quiet. Finally, I'd found a threat that worked on them.

"Now," I said, "What about that gasoline." The General was sloshing it back and forth with his agitator. Then he tipped his tub sideways and mumbled something about "pleasant bouquet" and "good legs." Then he swallowed. Then he belched.

"It's fine," he said. "Tell Murray the Mower he's sweet, and to drink up." The General burped again, and sent the mixture of water and gasoline down the drain. On the way up the stairs, I thought to myself: Did he say sweet?

I hurried back out to the shed, informed Murray the Mower of The General's conclusions, and began to dump gasoline into his tank.

"Say there," he said, "I have another question." Another question? That's not good. It was time to mow, not talk.

"Go ahead."

"Will you drive me in the gay parade this 4th of July?"

§

Same Sex

There's a lot of controversy currently surrounding the issue of whether or not same-sex marriages should be legalized, but I've felt safe because that issue doesn't follow me home. At least here, such issues as same-sex marriages are overshadowed by the frozen septic system drain field, the dentist's bill, and a new pair of shoes that hurt my feet.

So it was with some dismay that General Electric the Washing Machine, called me down to the basement last night in his normal fashion—he walked clear to the end of his hoses and sent clanking sounds of unbalanced discontent up the stairs.

I hurried down there. He is, after all, a general, and he can be a problem. I really wish Sir Nautilus the Water Heater would have taken command of the army of appliances in the basement. He's noble born, very soft spoken, and extremely political. He is pretty timid, though, and he still wets the floor when you upset him.

So I'm stuck with General Electric. I asked him what in the heck he thought he was doing, hopping around in a six-foot circle (the length of his hoses) like a maniac.

"You know what I was doing," he crisply replied, as he spat soap fluff and water out onto the floor. The general could be a real pain in the butt.

No, I don't. What is it exactly that you're doing?

"Trying to get your attention, Mr. President, that's what I was doing." It's not good when General E. calls me Mr. President. He knows I like it, and I know that he only does it when he's sucking up.

You've got my attention, I told him as I popped his hat off and looked at his wiring to see if he'd come loose down in there anywhere. Too bad we can't do that with real generals.

"I heard a rumor," he said.

What kind of rumor, I asked?

"The kind I don't like to hear," he said. "Rumors destroy armies; loose lips sink ships; a penny saved is a penny ......"

Ok, I said, hold on. (When he gets like that, you have to rein him in, or you'll be listening to platitudes all day.) I asked him to detail the rumors.

"I heard you're replacing Lady Kenmore the Dryer," he said.

Well, she burns my socks and won't run when I want her to, I said. Furthermore, I added, she's temperamental three weeks out of four, and won't work for company on the weekends.

Yeah," the General agreed, "she's a real pain in the butt." Now I know there's something going on. He's never that agreeable.

So what's the deal, I asked him. I found myself thinking this house used to be such a quiet little place.

"Well, here's the deal: I'm afraid you're going to go out and buy another Lady Kenmore."

I don't get it. Why do you care?

"I care because I'm getting kind of tired of her moods, and I think it's negatively affecting morale here in the Appliance Service." I still didn't get it. Usually, he gets even by sending Lady Kenmore extra wet clothing and towels, which takes her three times as long to tumble the moisture out of. I think it's the big reason her lungs are nearly shot.

So, what do you want me to do?

"Well, I don't want you to bring home another female dryer." Here, I swear, if a washing machine can wring his hands instead of a load of clothes, he was.

You're pretty riled up about all this, aren't you?

"You go through life thinking you've got all the answers," General E. told me, "then something happens to kind of wake you up, and then you see what's been pretty obvious all along." Maybe he saw it, but I sure didn't.

What is it exactly we're talking about?

General E. said: "I'm gay, and I want a dryer named Roper, or Amana. I want a guy dryer." I looked at him. The way he was holding his hoses looked pretty determined.

You're gay? I asked him. Oofda almighty! I wasn't sure what to say.

Wait! I said to him. What ever happened to Clinton's "don't ask; don't tell" policy for the military? Maybe I need a little of that myself about now.

"Beats me," the General said. "All I know is, I'm here, my gears are queer, and I'm proud of it."

OK, I told him. I'll shop for a guy dryer. I know when I'm licked. Then I asked him: Is there anything else?

"Yeah. Could you marry us?"

§

Water Heaters

I hate water heaters. I never met one that I liked. As a lot, they are an unruly bunch; individually, they rob their owners and pick on servicemen. In the many years that have passed since they and I first discovered our mutual dislike, we've been feuding. They're winning. They always win. Whoever controls the hot water in our modern society always wins.

They win a lot. Their water leaking, pilot-outing, mustache scorching, burned-out-element antics are hard to keep up with.

"Go on out to Sadie Whatshername," said my boss to me back on the first job I had up here. "Take a look at her water heater."

I'd been a TV repairman, had lots of electronic training—heck, this didn't seem like a fair contest, me vs. a simple electric water heater.

I realized when I stumbled going down an unfamiliar stairs that they, water heaters, can see in the dark, down there in the basement. I fell the last three steps, into a painful tangle of arms, legs, and spilled wrenches.

The water heater said, "Hey? You ok? You the guy thinks he can fix me? Can't even walk? Mr. Big Shot? Never met a schematic you couldn't follow? Think you're ready for me?"

Add sarcastic and condescending to my list of reasons why I don't like water heaters.

I searched in the dark for this fellow who was taunting me. I swept the surrounding walls with my hands, hoping for a light switch. I found cobwebs as I groped my way around in the basement, lost. Evidently what they say about the lost walking in circles is true. I made a circle and tripped over my scattered tools, and as I fell, I felt one hand sweep two Mason jars off a shelf next to me. They shattered on the floor like bombs. The water heater snickered.

It hadn't been like this with televisions. They were always upstairs, in rooms with windows and lights and people who were eager to lead me to the set, so they could watch Gilligan's Island. A home with a leaky television set could not be tolerated.

People never lead servicemen down to the basement. That's because they're afraid of what's down there. It doesn't matter that the folks that live there haven't showered in several days—they leave notes that say: "The door's open. If you need me, I'm in the living room watching Oprah." Then they'll add: "Excuse the messy basement." They can't clean down there because the water heater might get them.

In the process of wind milling around the basement, I found a light bulb, which I screwed in. It gave off about twenty watts, and yes, the basement was a mess. In the dimness, I tried to plug my trouble light into the light socket's receptacle, and couldn't.

All trouble lights have a polarized plug—one blade larger than the other. Light sockets don't. I think that's because they're also afraid of seeing the water heater. Anyway, the polarized socket is there to prevent…What is it there to prevent? Someone seeing the enemy?

I approached the rusty old electric water heater. Boy! They sure are long lived. I gingerly removed the inspection covers with my screwdriver, which I dropped. It rolled over into the corner under a moldy old mattress, two broken lamps, and a dehumidifier that hadn't worked in this century.

I thought I saw a loose screw terminal in the water heater. I reached my screwdriver in and BAAAZZZAATTTT!!!

I flung myself backward from the solar flare of my screwdriver slipping and shorting 240 volts to ground. I landed on the mattress, blind, with a fireworks display of great balls of yellow and red cascading across my retinas. Can you say "ocular trauma?" After several minutes of stargazing, I looked at my screwdriver. It was a lot shorter.

"You bit the end off my favorite screwdriver, Water Heater!"

"You shouldn't have stuck it in my face, Mr. Smart Guy," replied the water heater.

I pulled my voltmeter from a pocket, and approached the water heater again. I wasn't paying attention and tripped over a pile of National Geographics. I put out a hand to catch myself and stuck it right into the 240 volt terminals.

Electrocution isn't so bad, really, just a bunch of your muscles contracting in rhythm to the pulse of alternating current, kind of like birds flying around in your arm. Luckily, I was falling, so my hand came loose, and once again, found myself lying on the mattress.

They give shocks to crazy people, because it feels so darned good when it quits. I felt really good, and warm, too. Then I realized the warm was wet. I looked. The water heater was peeing on me.

I hate water heaters.

§

Annual Physical

As you may remember, when last I went down into the basement to attempt to mollify some of the unhappinesses that seem to be running rampant down there amongst The Appliance Group, it seemed almost hopeless.

General Electric the Washing Machine is boss down there, as much as anyone can be the boss. Apparently with advancing age his hoses are getting soft and his water, as he puts it, "doesn't splatter the tub anymore." Along with that, of course, his guts have slowed down to such a glacial pace that the clothes which he sends to Lady Kenmore the Dryer aren't wrung out.

"I think I'm constipated," he blurted out during his spin cycle as I addressed these issues with him. He was grunting a bit as the load inside him seemed never to finish. It embarrasses him to talk about his ailments, I know it does. He flips up his lid and whispers to me in order that Lady Kenmore the Dryer won't hear what he's saying.

Lady Kenmore herself isn't any spring chicken anymore. In fact, she's right in the midst of dryopause, and has become pretty hard to get along with. That's something new for her, because all these years, she's been the queen of the basement down there. "I was hot when I was young," she is wont to say. "I could handle men's underwear with the best of them." Then she could. Now, she's convinced that Mr. Williamson the Furnace is trying to incinerate her. "It's so hot in here," she says over and over as she keeps lowering the setting on her heating elements. I've had loads of laundry that would have dried faster hanging outside in the rain.

General Electric himself isn't a young pup anymore either, and each year when I give him his check-up—I'm a registered appliance doctor—he gets more and more apprehensive about what I'll find.

When I ask him if anything in particular is bothering him, he'll say: "Nope. I'm as healthy as a horse." He'll snicker and then say, "Well, a half a horsepower, you know."

So, how is your motor, General?" (I know it's pretty good, but he feels good if I ask him.)

"It's good," he'll say, then he'll add: "I'm not as good as I once used to be." Then he'll snort and say, "But I'm as good once as I ever was."

You're feeling pretty good, then? You'd say? (He's stalling. He knows what's coming.)

"Absolutely. I'm battle ready."

Good. You know the drill. Flip your front cover up and bend over.

"Ooooh no. I didn't think you were going to do that every year."

Well, now you're over fifty in people years (One human year is ten appliance years), it's recommended, you know, every year. Come on. Flip it up. Turn your head. Cough.

He hates the digital pump examination, where I, well, you know.

Lady Kenmore snickered and said, "That's nothing. You should have to put your feet up into some stirrups and see how you like that!"

Oh, I said, are you anxious for your annual oil smear, Lady Kenmore? (That usually shuts her door.)

General Electric the Washing Machine took a shot at distracting me by pointing out the window and saying, "Say, I think John Deere the Riding Mower is smoking."

I hate smoking. The General knows that. I looked out the window and The General slammed his inspection panel on my head. "Oops," he said. Yeah, oops. I rubbed the knot that was forming on my skull and said, "You did that on purpose." Over the years I've been sliced, pinched, slapped by belts…

"Ooooo, you've been slapped by belts?" That was Mr. Williamson, who has decided to come out of the closet. He also seems able to read minds. "Can I do that to you?" Then he said, "Will you do that to me? Belt me?"

Toshiba the 60 Inch Asian Television piped in about there by saying, "Can I watch?" He's turned out to be kind of perverted about stuff, and frequently, while I'm watching Discovery, he'll switch over to the Playboy Channel, to which I don't subscribe. All I see is swirling snow, but I can hear him humming happily to himself and saying things like: "Oh boy. That's a good frequency there, look at those sine waves on her, would you." I guess that means that he can see it.

"Look," I said to Mr. Williamson, "you'll get your belt when your old one wears out, or you know what will happen, right?" He knows alright.

The General said, "He'll have you by the nozzle if you don't watch out."

I hate giving physicals.

§

General Electric the Washing Machine Has a Diaper

General Electric the Washing Machine was coughing so hard that I could hear him clear upstairs. That tubby gut of his was acting like a megaphone. The floor was vibrating at seismic levels detectable clear to the coast. I raced down the stairs.

It was a dark night. I turned on the laundry room light, ignored the disarray of clothes scattered all around. Up there on the wall over The General, there was a line to which was attached an odd assortment of socks. Back a couple of years, I nailed that clothes line to the wall behind General Electric the Washing Machine, and hanging from it were every orphan stocking I found when I cleaned the room up.

I figure I'll give the room a couple more years of disarray to cough up the matches to those socks on the wall, and then I'll clean it again. I call that collection of socks the SMIA (socks missing in action) line.

In the meantime, I was shocked when I turned on the light. General Electric the Washing Machine was as white as a ghost. "Are you alright?" I asked him.

Stupid question. People are good at stupid questions. I was once in a car accident, broke my nose, had blood all over me. The first thing a passing motorist who stopped said was: "Are you alright?"

General Electric the Washing Machine let out another snort. He was not alright. Water sprayed out from beneath him on two different sides. His voice came out in gurgles, like he was talking through a tube partially filled with water: "Where are all these baby clothes coming from?" ("Gurgle, gurgle.") He said that.

I said: "You're dying, and you're wondering about baby clothes?"

He said: "I'm dying because of the baby clothes." He gurgled again, said: "I think there's a diaper stuck in my lower intestine."

He's such a hypochondriac. However, this time, maybe he's right. My daughter, her husband, and their daughter, who is seven months old, are spending some time here until fall comes, and a university teaching position opens up.

"You don't have a lower intestine," I said. Well, he does, kind of. Something must connect that tub of a gut of his to The Septic System.

I asked him: "Where does it hurt?" Then I poked him a good one in his drain hose, to see if it had prolapsed. I told him what every doctor has ever told me. "Hey. You're gonna feel some slight pressure." Someday, I'm going to look up in some medical text exactly what "pressure" means, and what I think I'll find is it's medical speak for "HURTS LIKE HELL!"

General Electric said: "Ouch! What'd you do that for? That hurt!"

"Ok, that's good. Numbness there would indicate something very bad."

"I'm leaking from several different places all at once," The General gurgled, "how can anything else be worse?"

That told me I had to go in. "OK," I warned him, "suck in your tub, I'm going to have to pop you open, and I don't want to be hurt by any buttons flying out at me under high pressure."

I popped his front cover, and found several other places to poke.

"Ouch!"

"Ugh!"

"Ooof!"

I stood back up, and asked him: "Do you want the good news or the bad news?"

He thoughtfully scratched his chinny console with his lid, and said: "Give me the good news, first."

Sure. "Hey, Sears has washing machines on sale."

He didn't think that was funny.

I gave him the bad news, then. "It's your pump."

"Oooooh no, not my pump." He was distraught. He began to wring his water hoses.

"Don't do that. You keep that up," I told him, "you'll spring a leak sometime when I'm not here, and you'll flood The Septic System." One thing everyone in here realizes is, you don't mess with him. Even Sir Nautilus the Water Heater, who routinely wets the floor because President Bush upsets him so much, is careful just how many tears of frustration he leaks out at one time. You send too much water to The Septic System, he shuts down, and everyone is up poop the creek.

"Yes, your pump." I felt bad for him. He knew what was coming. I was going to have to unplug him, flatline him for however long it took to do a pump transplant. That meant a live hose bypass, and the possibility that the twenty or so gallons of water held up above the pump in his high-capacity gut tub might bleed out.

"Look," I told him, "I've done a hundred of these, and once the new pump is in, you'll feel like a young machine again, and maybe, I get in there, I'll find it's just a blockage. I'll clear that out, get you right back in business."

The rest of the appliances, sensing a weakness in the leadership, started singing "For he's a jolly good fellow." They're such a sympathetic bunch. I told them to cut that out. They kept singing.

"I have to get you back in shape. There are lots of diapers coming your way."

He fainted.

I unplugged him and got my tools. A good faint is better than a general anesthetic.

§

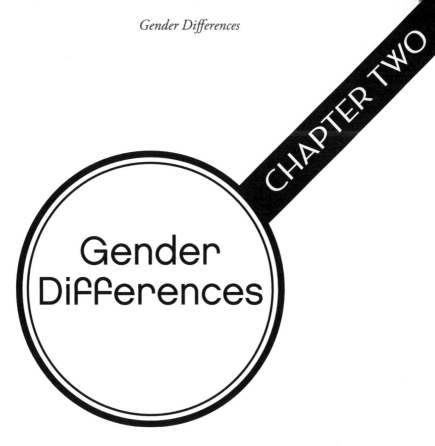

CHAPTER TWO

Gender Differences

Baby Picture Lesson

This happened in church, where everyone was sitting around individual tables enjoying coffee and eats before the service actually started. It was quite crowded already when I got there, and there wasn't any room at the big kids' table (other guys, talk about chain saws, animals, politics). So, I sat down between a lady and a young girl. The young girl was maybe 16. The lady left, then I chatted with the young girl a bit, which was easy. She was thinking about her future, and what she wanted to do.

Someone at the next table over handed our table a photo, which the young girl in turn took, examined, and then offered to me. I took it, looked at it. It was a baby picture. I handed it back to the young girl, smiled at her, and said: "I've got some great advice for you."

She gave me the amount of attention a grown-up sitting next to her in a crowd deserved, which meant she was at least looking at me. That's often more than you get from a teenager, but then, I wasn't her parent.

I said, as I handed it back to her, "Handing a picture of a week-old baby to a guy is very complicated." I was watching her. She seemed interested. What a faker this kid was.

"First," I went on, "If you can help it, never hand a picture of a week-old baby to a guy, unless the baby is sitting either on a tractor or a motorcycle or in a 1958 Corvette convertible." It doesn't even matter if the red-faced, chubby-cheeked, wrinkled-up little demon was fathered by the guy, guys don't want to look at baby pictures. Guys don't understand baby pictures. Guys don't understand babies. They haven't carried it cramped up against their bladder for nine months; they haven't felt it kicking the snot out of their internal organs; they haven't looked forward their entire adult lives to having one. In short, guys just don't get babies.

Once the kid is old enough to play catch, or spit, or pull the dog's hair, that's different.

All this the young girl listened to pretty attentively. Pretty impressive.

"But," I said, "there are times when you might want to hand a guy a picture." Such a move would be a kind of test, I told her, one in which you want to know more about the guy.

"Two things will happen," I went on. "First, the guy will do exactly what I did." I looked at it for traces of tractors or guns or something interesting, which took exactly one-tenth of a second, and handed it back. Next item of business, please, let's move things along here.

"I'm sure what confused you is the fact that I sat down at this table where several women are sitting, and began to chat with you all." I went on to point out that that didn't mean I was one, but that I needed a place to sit. It's hard to eat standing up.

She said: "What was the other thing." I blinked. She was actually paying attention.

"The other thing. The other thing." I blinked twice. Lately, these geezer moments are coming faster. The young girl waved the baby picture at me. Somewhere deep down in the freezer I'm using for a brain a connection remade.

"Oh yeah, the other thing," I stumbled, grabbing for it desperately.

And then I had it. I pounced on it, brought it to the surface, and said: "If you do choose to hand a baby picture to some guy, and he looks at it and says something like: 'Ooooooo, cute baby,' then don't trust that guy. He wants something, something you've got." I smiled somewhat knowingly, raised my eyebrows at her to see if she understood, and she nodded. Just to make sure, I said: "Never trust a guy who oooo's and aaaaa's at a baby picture. It isn't natural."

A guy like that is either a sissy, or confused about his gender, or a no-good up to something. At any rate, something's off.

"But," I finally said, "if you hand a baby's picture to a guy and he does exactly what I did," which was to grunt and hand it back, "then you can trust him, because he isn't putting up a front for anyone, and likely, he'll tell you exactly what he's thinking, whether or not you like it,."

A good looking blond woman came, sat down on my left, and said: "What's happening?"

I turned to her, fell into the deepest blue eyes I've ever seen, handed her the baby picture, and said: "Now there's the cutest baby I've ever seen."

I looked at the young girl. Winked. Something in my eye.

§

Men Have Needs

An article in a recent farmers' magazine was titled: "Men have specific needs to make marriage happy." Several needs, in fact, as the author wax-on, wax-offed his way through this marital minefield.

First on the list was for the wife to be "less critical." Wonderful idea. Impossible. Some other impossible "lesses" might be: "a woman less pregnant;" "a bank account less broke;" "a tire less flat."

Less critical isn't going to cut it. A house on fire can be less on fire and still be on fire. A woman less critical is like standing next to a million-degree fire wishing it was only a hundred thousand degrees instead.

Less critical is good; UN-critical is what men want, as in the following:

"That's a nice new motorcycle you've just brought home there, dear."

"I can mow the lawn with that old push mower just fine, don't you worry, dear."

"I really like your hair—did you really cut it yourself?"

"I never did think men needed to wear underwear."

This author goes on to say: "Men have their own needs, and often feel on the defensive." Defensive? We're not defensive! He's got no right saying that!
This guy knows what he's talking about. Here's another one of those "less ain't better enough" deals. Less defensive isn't going to cut it. Less defensive would be for the wife to say: "If you think I'm mowing the yard one more time with that old mower, we need to talk." This is compared to the more likely utterance: "If you think we're going to mow the yard while you go fishing again, then the next thing you're going to think about will be my backside going down that driveway with the kids, both cars, and a lawyer."

You want the perfect, UN-defensive-provoking remark? It's: "While you're fishing, the kids and I are going to walk to the neighbors and borrow their lawnmower and some gas and mow the yard. It'll be fun." A guy could fish defense-guilt free.

Next point: Men shouldn't be criticized for not knowing what their wife is thinking, when the wife doesn't say anything about any of it.

This one might be asking too much of the little woman, who has grown up with other little women, all of whom have tuned their touchy-feely facial-expression-interpreting skills to a razor edge on one another. There's a book in a raised eyebrow; a movie in a frown.

Meanwhile, little men have been finding little animals to squash while thinking little women are yukky. The only razor's edge they care about is on their knife, the better to carve their name somewhere. Their friend Billy busts his head open and then cries about it, he better watch out. They'll carve him up soon as not. Crybaby.

Given this upbringing, it's no wonder women think men "just don't get it," as the author points out.

They don't! On the other hand, women know deep down that they cannot limp into the house at the end of a long day, walk up to their husband and say: "I hate my hair—my life is ruined—I'm gonna ruin yours too." Husbands would die of shock. For the first time, a husband told that would know why she was making him miserable.

But the woman cannot tell him that. If she did, he would say: "It'll grow out," and go back to draining the oil out of his tractor all over the flowerbed, thinking to himself how grateful he is that it's nothing serious.

Oh, it's serious, make no mistake about that. It's real serious. It's why authors write about this stuff.

Finally, this author says that a good wife will forget the past, and leave past hurts and "blunders" alone. Blunders? Now, there's a great word. Notice that when the word "blunder" comes up, no one thinks of females. Females don't blunder. Most men spend their entire lives wishing they had a woman who could blunder. Men understand blunderers. Admittedly, they don't think this stuff through very well. "Dear," the little woman says to her husband when he comes in out of the field, "I think something went wrong with the skid loader hydraulics when I tried to move that big rock behind the barn that the cattle have been stumbling over."

Awwww. She cares. Then the next day the bill for the repairs comes. "Good grief, woman," he says to her, "couldn't you just make my life miserable instead of blundering around like a guy?"

One blunderer to a house, that's my motto.

Women'll just have to adjust.

§

Tears

Response was almost measurable to a recent column concerning the fact that females never apologize. That somewhere around the age of first learning to speak, there is an upsurge of behavior in females that should bear the label of "neverus sorrious."

It's a fact that one husband was chasing his wife around the yard with last week's copy of that particular newspaper in his hand, hollering: "See? See?"

He couldn't catch her. She's in better shape than he is. In any hell-bent-for-leather footrace down the road, my money's on her. You go, girl.

When it comes to apologizing, though, the real money's on the guy.

So, women never apologize, and that's a true edge. They don't have too, however, because they have complete, real-time control of their tear ducts. Real women are as much in control of their tear ducts as plumbers are of a flush toilet.

Women would like men to think that, completely opposite to the statement above, they have no control over their water works whatsoever. Nope. There are a few definite categories that seem to surface repeatedly, when it comes to various situations involving crying. Females develop this early on in life, once they find out where it works, which is on males. Think back: Did you ever witness tears working intrafemaley? You know, one woman giving any credence to another woman's tears?

That's because all women are in on this. I've seen one woman sit and calmly drink coffee while another woman was snotting up two or three boxes of Kleenex, just waiting for the deluge to end so they could talk about whatever was the problem. They know that there's always a chance some male might pop into the kitchen inadvertently, and just in case that happens, there should be a good sob in process. Once they see that there's no chance of any male popping up, then they'll get on with whatever it is they're getting on with.

There ain't a man in the world who could do that, just sit there like that, and watch a woman cry. We've been indoctrinated since birth not to just sit there like a bump on a log, feeling useless, out of it, no clue what's going on. We can't sit there because our upbringing concerning tears was whispered to us beginning in the womb. There's a book for expecting mothers. It's titled: "Things you need to say to your unborn baby about female tears."

On page one, it says: "In case your child might be a boy, whisper these words to your belly at least one hundred times: 'Never fail to take action when a woman is crying, because only someone dumb as dirt would just sit there.'" Action, that's what this crying stuff is all about. It's ingrained into males.

Men? Isn't this true? Tell the truth: You cannot just sit there and let a female cry, can you?

Kings have fallen on their swords out of frustration with the queen's tears. Great artists have opened their veins at their inability to solve their true love's weeping. Dictators have resigned over their wife's unhappiness.

One factory worker was so upset over his wife's crying that he went out and shot the end of his finger off, so upset was he that he didn't notice that, as he was sighting his rifle in, he couldn't see that finger through the scope. So it's not just kings.

Women are great situational criers. A classic example is one where the husband walks in the door after a hard day, and his wife is holding up two swim suits, one a bikini, the other a one-piece. "Which one do you like the best?"

Lord help the husband faced with this dilemma. No matter what answer he gives or what logic he attaches to that answer, tears are going to flow.

You know why? Because this doesn't have anything to do with the swim wear; it has to do with the fact that females know what works, and what doesn't, and the guy now knows she wants something. He'll at first think it's like a new blender, or a nice toaster, or maybe out to the ChatterBox Café for a steak burger. When her tears get worse, he'll eventually figure out that this one isn't going to be so easy.

It'll be her job to keep the tears real enough that eventually he'll get around to whatever it is she's getting around to.

About that, men don't have a clue.

Real men never know.

§

Women: Things They Shouldn't Start the Conversation With

The words "you're probably not going to like this" were still echoing in my head when I turned back to the woman who had said them—a young single mother who rents a house from me-- and said: "You know what? Never start a conversation with a man by saying, 'You're probably not going to like this.'" Where has this chick been? Where was the mother hen who should have passed this information on to her?

.   Is there a worse way to start a conversation with a man? It's doubtful. One worse way might be to run up to me with a fire extinguisher in her hand just as I drive in to the property she rents from me and shout at me: "Look out! It's going to blow!"

But even that's not so bad. Not really. At least I know what the danger is, and how timely the ensuing detonation is going to be. Guys like information like that. Information about pending fireworks demonstrations is always welcome. With information like that, we can cover our ears to protect them, watch a good explosion, and enjoy the low deductibles on our new insurance policy.

I'll tell you what's worse: Some significant female in your life meets you at your door and says, "We have to talk." Oh boy. Wasn't life good just a moment ago? That's a distinct step toward one of you turning into the "insignificant" other, and I'll give you two guesses which one of you it will be.

But to say: "You're not going to like this," well, that's way too open-ended a threat. It could mean any one of a thousand dreadful things. It could mean: A dentist is coming and he's going to drill that molar right here in the yard, with no Novocain. Or, you my renter is a prophet, and you just got a premonition of how I'm going to die, but you don't know exactly when. Or, you my renter is a doctor, and that tiny mark on my face is upper Japanese river melanoma, I've got two weeks to live. Or, you might say to me: "Remember that time you got drunk and thought you met the love of your life in a bar. Guess what? It was …." STOP! STOP! STOP!

PLEASE! DON'T DO THIS TO ME! NO MORE! NO MORE! I CAN'T TAKE ANY MORE OF THIS NOT KNOWING! IT'S PROBABLY GOING TO BE AWFUL! I DON'T WANT TO GO ON LIVING WITH THIS TERRIBLE FATE HANGING OVER ME!

I don't think women begin to realize how precariously balanced we men are at heart. No, I'm not talking about various bodily injuries we've done to ourselves. Men ride bulls, jump off bridges, court disaster at the drop of the hat. Guys cut two fingers off with a power saw and don't even think twice about it. Hah! Most men would cut two fingers off just to have two fingers cut off. Then we could walk into a bar, count out money with that hand just so someone will ask: Wow. What'd you do with your fingers?"

So then you could proudly reply, "Oh, not much. I was hanging upside down from that big oak branch outside the bedroom window so's I could retrim the soffit cantilever with my Black and Bloody 4-horsepower 12-bladed high voltage saw which I bought from some guy's widow at a garage sale for two bits. Just then a coreolis tornado slammed me up against a rogue piece of balloon framing. When I came to, the fingers were gone." You count out the money. You say, "No big deal."

But have a woman come up to you and say, "You're probably not going to like this," and now what have you got? Absolutely nothing. No guy walks into a bar and proudly boasts: "Some woman just talked to me and scared me so bad that I almost peed my britches." Nothing.

So here, ladies. Here's an example situation you might find yourselves in and if you do, what you say to the significant male other in your life, assuming, that is, that your main goal at that moment in time isn't to give him a coronary or a sudden heart stoppage.

Through no fault of your own, you told the neighbor, "Sure, it's fine. He won't mind if you use his tractor." Later, the neighbor calls and tells you that there's something wrong with the tractor and as soon as it's pulled out of the lake he'll let you know.

Your husband-significant other comes in the door, home from work. You say: "I'll buy you a new tractor I loaned yours to the neighbor I'm so stupid I love you whip me beat me make me write bad checks."

Try it.

But not, "You're probably not going to like this."

§

Women: Sensitivity Award at the Library

The pretty young woman at the library handed me back the book I was checking out. She had affixed a sticky note to it, which said: "DO NOT DESENSITIZE."

Do not desensitize? Being as how I'm a male raised by a female, trained by a Tribe of Girls, cautioned for years about sexual bigotry in the workplace, and in general afraid to be in a room full of women for fear of drowning in a sea of estrogen, it caught my eye.

I'm afraid of drowning. Do not desensitize? I thought quickly, frantically. Was this a prank? I looked at the door, my way out. I glanced at the librarian, as she went to help another patron. Nope. She didn't seem unduly involved, as she would have been had she said to someone, likely another female: "Now, watch this. I'm going to give the next guy who comes in a sticker that says "Do not desensitize" and see what happens."

Had this been the case, they'd have been over in the corner enjoying my discomfiture. Which they weren't.

Does this warning mean that I'm too sensitive? That, finally, after a lifetime of women accusing me of, among other things, being not sensitive to their whims and wishes, they've recognized my advances in this field? That, maybe, at the last meeting of The Tribe of Girls, someone stood up and made the motion: "He's been doing real good at reading our minds and remembering birthdays, let's give him a sticker."

All in favor, etc., etc., and although I picture the vote as close, I eked one out.

Lord knows, I've had my trouble figuring out what women want. For example, once, some women friends visited and stayed the night. Just before bedtime, one of them said: "I see that living out in the country poses a lot of wildlife issues."

Oh, yes, I said, it certainly does, blithely babbling on about foxes and eagles and whatnot, all the while watching them become more and more uneasy as bedtime approached and they were to head for their assigned bedroom.

Well, I watched them, but I didn't see. I wrote all this off to their excitement at spending the night in the same house with someone as charming and sophisticated as me. This is a classic example of the old, un-sensitive me. I didn't pick up on the looks exchanged between them, the little wordless communications that I now, being the winner of a desensitizer award, realize exist, but didn't know about back then.

It was six months later when one of them, in a telephone conversation, asked about my house being overrun with mice: "All those mousetraps all over the house," she said, "we were afraid to go to bed."

Oh.

Had I been the mind reader then that I am now, I would have intercepted these brain waves and replied: "Those are just to keep the cat from climbing in the flower pots."

I told her that. Silence on the other end. I'm going to guess, judging from that silence and my new-found higher sensitivity, that it wasn't her that made the sensitivity award nomination.

Really, though, I have been trying hard. Why, just the other day, when the young woman at the grocery store asked me: "Paper or plastic?", I replied, "What would you like, please." There, I thought to myself, that's the new sensitive me in action.

I guess she didn't really know. Well, I know she didn't know, or she wouldn't have asked me to make up her mind for her. I just thought that she should have more say in the decision, which is what I told her. Then I said: "Life is just one big mousetrap, isn't it?" Then I gave her my best most understanding look, and winked at her. Yes, I know, I wanted to tell her, making one's own decisions are difficult, but I'm on your side.

The cashier at the till, an older woman, suddenly looked ill. That happens, you know. It's winter. One minute you feel well; the next, you're coming down with some-thing. The new sensitive me asked: "There's a lot of stuff going around, isn't there?"

She gave me an understanding look. Boy, she sure agreed, apparently.

Glad I could help, I wanted to tell her, but she seemed to know that already.

I looked once again at the "DO NOT DESENSITIZE" sticker. Then at the librarian. I got her attention, and asked her: "Is this for me?"

"Well," she replied, "kind of. Otherwise, you'll set off the alarm when you leave."

I waved at her. "Thank you very much." She seemed confused.

Well. I had no idea. Technology has progressed to the point at which they are measuring sensitivity.

"Good luck," I said to the guy just entering as I was leaving.
He'd need it.

§

Women: We Need to Talk

Perhaps I was wrong some time ago when I speculated that the worst words a guy can hear at the beginning of a conversation with a woman are for her to say: "I've got bad news." In fact, I've changed my mind; they're not the worst at all. They're bad, but the worst—the ones that really that strike abject fear into the male heart, are: "We need to talk."

Except for a couple of examples and some narrative to flesh all this out, most guys will agree with me that this subject really doesn't need much more discussion; that this is all they want to hear about it, let's go clean manure out of the calf pen or get that root canal taken care off—something more fun.

"I've got bad news" does in fact seem to be the standard conversation opening gambit employed by anyone possessing one or more ovaries. The first thought that pops up here is: Do they use this on one another, woman to woman? Or is this particular little combination of words solely used with males, through some mistaken belief that it shows a certain respectful trepidation of mechanical things? Kind of an I-don't-know-what-the-big-deal-is-but-I'm-cool-with-machines feeling. That's usually where it's used, as in: "I've got bad news, the red light is on in the car."

Him: Well, dear, maybe it isn't so bad. (His guts are twisting up into knots. It's bad. Other Guys will make fun of him.) How long has it been on?

Not too long, maybe since the girls and I went to Fargo last week? Is that long?

Well, dear, maybe not. (Omigod since Fargo. That crankshaft will be scrap.)

Her: I don't see why we need a red light to tell us to put windshield washer fluid in anyway.

IT"S THE WINDSHIELD WASHER FLUID LIGHT? NOT THE OIL LIGHT?

Uh huh. Why? Does that matter?

There you have it, the typical conversation with a woman that has opened with the "I've got bad news" warning. One really has to think they're just trying to connect, even though they don't have a clue how terrifying are the results of mechanical malfeasance to a male. They want to be perceived as sympathetically involved in this world of machinery and moving parts. (Mechanical malfeasance means ignoring the messages from The Machine Gods, messages that often come in forms as varied and incomprehensible as a good Evangelist speaking in tongues. Knocking, whistling, squeaking, rattling, squealing, and just generally altered behavior are the conventional means by which The Message comes that your car, your furnace, your snow mobile, etc., is about to poop the big one.)

Women don't generally acknowledge these messages. They rely instead on faith and patience with The Machine Gods; that those squeaks and vibrations are mere tests of faith, and mean nothing more; that if women as machine operators are patient and nurturing, the knocks and shakes won't get worse.

"I've got bad news," therefore, mostly involves things with two or more moving parts.

Which brings us to what appear to be the really terrifying words with which women open up conversations with men: "We need to talk."

Boys, one thing is for certain: Any conversation with a member of the opposite sex that begins with those words is not going to pertain to machinery. Nope. It's going to involve a long and torturous discussion of stuff regarding COMMUNICATION, and RELATIONSHIP, and YOUR SHORTCOMINGS thereof.

An example is in order:

Her: We have to talk.

Him: AAAIIIIEEEEEGGGGGGHHHH!!!!!!! (The screams fade as this particular guy runs off into the local cave, or the local bar, whichever is closest, a bar being the closest thing to a cave that we have since dark and deep caves went out of fashion.)

Let's try again: Her: We have to talk.

Him: What did I do now? (Sound familiar? Conversations that women begin with WHTT (We have to talk) never involve a woman's shortcomings. Just his. Just to prove this:

Her: WHTT.

Him: Uh huh. What about?

Her: I made a mistake and I'm sorry. I'll be your slave forever.

Yeah, right! That ain't gonna happen, see what I mean.

Here's what is gonna happen. Her: WHTT.

Him: Ooookkkaaayyyy. (He's looking out the window for an escape route.)

Her: You remember Ann, the lady I introduced you to in church the other day? She just moved back to town?

Him. Hmmmm. (Keeping it noncommittal, until he can see which way the wind blows.)

Her. You never mentioned that you two went steady back in high school?

Him. (This is over. Maybe a quick bluff.) I didn't think it was important. (Guys, it really isn't, is it? To us. Really. Honest. Hardly remember those sessions under the football bleachers.)

Her. Wipe that silly look off your face. You're in big trouble here, mister. (She begins to cry. Oh, man. That's really cheating. You never follow WHTT with tears. WHTT always involves an argument, followed by two days of the silent treatment, and a slow glacier-paced thawing.)

Him. (Thinking fast, as the eternal instinct for survival kicks in.) She hates you, you know.

Her. (Momentarily distracted.) Why?

Him. Because you're thinner and better looking than she is.

This one is over. This guy remembered the magic words. But next time, he won't be so lucky.

Neither will you.

§

Women: Grocery Stores, and Asking For Directions

I usually do my grocery shopping as late at night as possible. There are a couple of reasons why: First, it's because of the aisles and poky, contemplative women who pause in front of the canned peas and study first the shelves and then several individual cans—each of which contain the apparent same thing, little round green vegetables. It's as though they were going to live forever and the fate of the known world depended upon their pea decision.

As I race up to these veggie worshippers in once again a failed bid to enter and leave the grocery store in a best personal time, I skid to a stop before them and take three milliseconds—other men are besting my time, you realize—to ponder their beatific facial expressions.

Does God live in the vegetable aisle? Oh, boy, what if he does, and I'm skipping on by Him because I think he lives in church, which is where most of us go to look for him.

Once, in a fit of participatory yearning, I too took a can of peas and beheld it, waiting for grace or lightning, or at least a peaceful interlude. The pea stack on the shelf collapsed and several cans crashed to the floor. The resulting chaos around me and my cart drew some let me tell you not very pleasant looks from the other pea worshippers. I fled, back the direction from which I came, and darted down the next aisle, which was full of soaps and detergents, a much more likely aisle, right? for Him.

Even at nine at night, some of the aisles are plugged with studious shoppers. Nonetheless, there are not as many, and if I'm going to set the world speed shopping record per item purchased, that's when it's going to happen, which is reason number two for being there at that time of night.

There I was, rolling through the store my smooth grab and snatch technique, the cart barely pausing while I filled it.

I noticed two young women more than once.

More than once needs some clarification, as does young women. First, at this point of my age, more women are young. That's kind of a neat thing, kind of, although I mention it at the risk of you getting the wrong idea about me having any kind of perverted regard for that younger segment of women. Let me say that it is an observation made merely from a neutral, viewer-based, scientific point of view, based on the fact that once, when I was, say, 16, there were not so many younger women around, like, hardly any.

Now there are. Enough said. One of the younger women was accompanied obviously by her daughter, who was younger yet, in the twenty-something bracket. I noticed them because one does not that often find mother-daughter shopping pairs in this age combination. I noticed them even further because as often as not, mom would pick something off the shelf, and, along with both of them contemplating it as though it were a diamond bracelet they had just discovered, now they were also discussing it. The first couple of times I made a high-speed 180-degree turn necessary to compete in this shopping race, they were down that aisle, and I had to veer over to the next one.

But they were in every aisle, and eventually, I accumulated a lot of—for one moving at this rate—observation time. After they discussed it at length, quite often the daughter would put the item back on the shelf, and drag the shopping cart away, leaving mom no choice but to come along. Ah, how roles change, eh? Not that long ago, it was the mom putting stuff back, and the little daughter hurrying after her.

I skidded around the cereal corner, saw that although they were in front of me, there was room to pass by. As I was passing by, the daughter turned to me and asked: "Do you know where the jars are?"

Her mom—whom I knew from somewhere—said: "But he doesn't work here."

The daughter said: "I know, but he looked like he knew what he was doing."

???????????

Really? Honest? No! Me?

I stopped, said hello, then said to the daughter: "Thank you. I think you've just scored a first for me, any woman, any time, any where, telling me I knew what I was doing."

I wanted to pull the mom aside and lecture her a bit about her falling short in educating her daughter in The Tribe of Girls protocol about all this, but I didn't. Instead, I said to the young woman: "Look. You have to know that if you're going to go through life thinking that at any time a man knows what he's doing, and actually telling him that, you've got a lot of heartache ahead of you."

Of course, I was smiling. I sped off, turned around after a few steps and said to her: "Thank you."

I was checking out, asked the clerk where the jars were just as the younger women were turning my end of another aisle, and told them what I was just told.

A man asking for directions is not normal. A woman? Normal.

A woman asking a man for directions?

Bless you, younger woman.

§

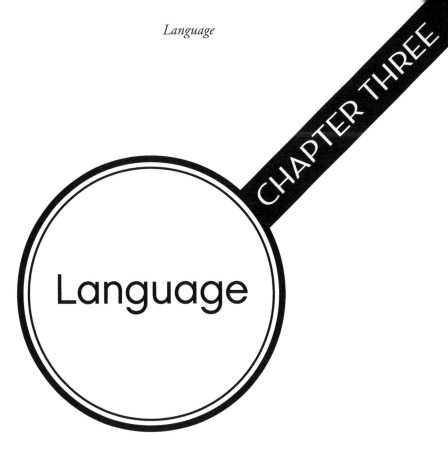

CHAPTER THREE

Language

English Language

Cut to the chase. Arm and a leg. Big wig. Crack a smile. Straight laced. We use these terms so casually that, as is often the case with the English language, we never even consider the origins of the phrases we often use.

Cut to the chase of course came from the first talkie movies, which were often westerns. The sure recipe for success here, since no one was talking, and all the communication was done either by sub titles or a person standing in front of the stage using a megaphone, was to get to the part where the good guys mount their horses and chase the bad guys. Cutting was what was done to the film.

Arm and a leg. Back in the days before photography, images of people could only be done as sculpture or painting. Just about everyone is familiar with those portraits of George Washington standing behind his desk, one arm behind his back. Others of him showed one hand in his coat. Still others showed all of his arms and legs. Prices charged by portrait painters back then were based on how many limbs were to be included in the portrait. Limbs of course are arms and legs, and were more difficult to paint than coats and shirts; therefore, they cost more. Hence the origin of the expression: "It'll cost you an arm and a leg."

Big wig. Back in the sixteenth century, people commonly bathed only a couple of times a year—just before winter; just after. Women often kept their hair covered, as was the style, with hats and scarves, but men—because of lice and a general disregard for style—shaved their heads. Privileged men wore wigs, as only the wealthy could afford wigs constructed of wool, which, because it was un-washable, presented a problem, To solve this, they carved a loaf of bread the size of their head, put it inside the wig, and baked the whole thing in an oven. The heat, and I suppose the moisture from the bread, would fluff the wig up nice and big. Hence, this is the origin of the expression: "He's a big wig."

Crack a smile. At about this same time in history, the lack of hygiene had a negative effect on one's complexion. Women would spread bee's wax over their facial skin to smooth out and treat their accumulated skin damage. While this would happen at the local women's parlors, if one woman were to stare overmuch at another woman, she might be told: "Mind your own bee's wax." Should a woman smile, the wax would crack, and that's where the expression "crack a smile" came from.

Back then, ladies wore corsets, and the ideal waist size was about 14 inches, believe it or not. That was the goal, anyway, and these corsets were laced up pretty tight, so tight that the wearer could not bend over, sit down, play cards, dance, walk, or even laugh. We now have the expression "straight laced" to refer to people who stiffly resist life's temptations. Resisting is easy when you cannot move.

Playing with a full deck came from early England, and referred to a tax levied on playing cards. To make the tax less offensive, the authorities only taxed the ace of spades. Those people who were so shortsighted as to refuse to pay the tax only bought 51 cards, and tried to play that way. People mostly thought this was pretty dumb, and we now extend this expression to other people we think are dumb, when we say "he's not playing with a full deck."

Words are fun.

§

Honeymoon

We're going to continue my love affair with the English language as we look into some more words that have arisen in my path over the last few weeks. The first word that caught my eye—or ear, I guess--came when a wife referred to her husband's expanding waist size as his new "girth."

I thought to myself—now, that's a word one doesn't hear much anymore. Girth. It's a nice sounding word that somewhat unfairly doesn't get to be used much any more. It's actually derived from a word in carpentry, girt, which refers to something that holds two corner posts together, or something like that. So that's kind of like something that holds your guts in, which girth kind of does.

As horse riders also know, girth is the strapping that holds the saddle on the horse's back.

Ah hah! Wife. Husband. Saddle. That has to be a connection. Connection or not, it's still a nice word.

The next new word that popped up in my path comes from an accepted practice way back 2000 years before the birth of Christ, when the new father-in-law was expected to supply his new son-in-law with all the mead the son could drink for the first month of his marriage. Mead of course is a liquor—kind of a beer made out of grain and honey—and was valuable back then because first, in the process of brewing itself, the bacterial process involved purified the water; and second, honey is just about the only food around that will not spoil, no matter how it is packaged, stored, ignored, so the drink made from it also kept well.

The fact that this "honor" of keeping your new son-in-law drunk fell to a parent who probably wanted the best for his daughter seems kind of paradoxical, in that if the daughter did find and marry an upstanding young man, still, all that booze for a month might turn out not to be the best thing. Maybe fathers were just protecting their daughters' chastity—get the guy drunk; keep him drunk.

Anyway, the new word is "honeymoon." Back then, time was measured against a calendar based on lunar cycles, and this month following the marriage was generally referred to back then as the "honey month." Hence, honeymoon. It definitely has a much better ring to it than, for example, whiskymoon, or Budweisermoon. Boozemoon. Comamoon.

It probably wouldn't be long before the new young bride got the groom aside, and told him to mind his p's and q's.

Which is the next term we're going to explain---p's and q's. This next word comes from booze also, and goes back to merry olde England, where, in the pubs, all beer and ale and whatever was sold in—guess what?—pints and quarts. Thus, when the patrons became drunkenly unruly, the bartender admonished them to "mind your p's and q's, or you'll have to leave."

There's more terminology that comes from these old inns and taverns. Back then, some patrons of pubs—who at that time carried their drinking vessel around with them—had their glazed clay mugs manufactured with a whistle built into the handle. Those patrons who minded their p's and q's were thus allowed to "wet their whistles," namely, to drink more booze, which they called for by blowing the whistle on their empty cup.

One other term, "the whole nine yards," is believed to originate back in this same era, when tall and fancy drinking glasses—which were something on the order of a couple of feet tall-- were referred to as "yards." Sailors just fresh into Liverpool from sailing the seven seas considered it quite necessary to hit all nine pubs that existed back then in Liverpool, and to drink a complete one of these at each pub, hence the term, "the whole nine yards" was born. That much booze, they probably couldn't even spell p or q.

Enough about booze. Let's talk about the condiment "ketchup," and where that term came from. It turns out that the Dutch were heavy users and importers of this stuff back in—you guessed it—the 1700's. It came from China, and wasn't even made from tomatoes back then. Instead, it was an Asian concoction of salted and spiced edible fungi (incidentally, in case you're not certain as to the pronunciation of that, the "gi" is soft, as in "ji.") such as mushrooms and smut (a mold that grows on corncobs which people consider a delicacy). The Chinese word for it was ke-tsiap, which the Dutch re-spelled to ketjap, which is pronounced just like we say it—ketchup.

Finally, the word "lady" goes way back, like to the seventh century in Old England, when it was spelled hladfdige. The "h" is silent; so is the "f." And the "ge." In the thirteenth century, the term changed to "levedi"; in the fourteenth, it changed to "levdi"; and finally to "ladie" and "lady" in the sixteenth.

What did it mean way back when? It referred to the woman who was the best bread maker in the castle, or village.

English is such a glorious language.

§

Raining Cats and Dogs

This is a column about the English language.

From early England, back in the early 1500s, we get a pretty interesting bunch of traditions and expressions. For instance, do you know why people now get married in June? That traces back to when civilization in the winter could not readily provide either a warm place to take a bath, or any way to easily warm the water to begin with. Along comes May. The river thaws, people bathe, good smelling young men and women do what they've done since time began, and when June comes, they still smell good enough to get married.

They didn't smell all that good. That's why brides carried bouquets of flowers.

Even bathing wasn't all that it was cracked up to be. Wait! "Cracked up?" Before we can use the English language to explain more about bathing, we have to deal with "cracked up." The word "crack" comes from archaic English. It used to mean a "burglar," somebody that took something.

Then the Navy got hold of it, and began to apply it to sailing ships which ran with full sail in high winds on high seas, and called it "cracking on." Usually there was one result of running full sail in those conditions: You cracked up. You broke your ship.

Bathing wasn't all that it was cracked up to be, because there was a hierarchy of bathing order. First came the man of the house, who got the nice clean water. Next, came other men of the house, after which came the sons. Finally it was the women's turn, and last of all came the babies. The water got pretty black from all the dirt and grime. This is where the expression: "Throwing out the baby with the bathwater" came from.

Olde merry England got a lot of rain. People lived in huts with roofs made of grass tied into bundles, or thatches, to keep the rain out. These thatches were piled high on a light timber framework. During cold weather, cats and dogs and other small animals burrowed into those roofs to keep warm. If it rained real hard, the grass became slippery. Hence the answer to the question: "How hard did it rain?" Well, it rained cats and dogs.

These roofs didn't hold much out. Many small bugs and mice fell through into the living area. This is the origin of canopy beds, because an old blanket or something kept falling rodents and bugs at least out of the bed, and onto the dirt floor.

The expression "dirt poor" came from this era, too, because wealthier people had stone, or slate, floors. If you didn't, you were dirt poor. Masonry floors got real slippery when the thatched roofs leaked, letting water in, or when garbage and meat scraps got strewn about. To correct this, folks threw straw–which was called "thresh"-- on the floor. As wet weather or winter drew on, and the thresh got deep, a board had to be installed across the bottom of the door opening to keep the thresh inside. That's where the term "thresh hold" came from.

Meat in those days was difficult if not impossible to come by; pork especially so. A slab of bacon was often hung inside as a sign of personal wealth for all visitors to see when they came over. The expression "bringing home the bacon" still describes someone who is successful at providing for others. If the visitor was truly welcome, he was given some fatty bacon to chew on, and that's where the expression "chewing the fat" came from.

During this era, plagues often swept through the country, and places to bury people became difficult to find. The people would dig up old graves, take the bones to a "bone-house" where they were stored, and reuse the old coffin and grave site.

One out of 25 of these wood coffins showed scratch marks on the inside, which meant that loved ones were occasionally buried alive. After that, when they buried someone, they tied a string around the wrist of the cadaver, and ran the string up above ground to a bell. Someone would then sit in the graveyard at night and listen for signs of life.

And that's where the expression "graveyard shift" came from.

And the expression "dead ringer."

And the expression "saved by the bell."

§

Ring Around the Rosie

As I was having coffee during fellowship hour at the church, the conversation turned toward old sayings. You know them—sayings like: "A penny saved is a penny earned"; "It's raining cats and dogs"; "It's cold enough to freeze the balls off a brass monkey (one of my favorites, which I did NOT bring up in church).

This turned into a round robin, where for a time, we exchanged sayings along with their meanings. "Raining cats and dogs" refers to a time in England when everyone lived in a little house with a roof made of thatched grasses. When it got cold outside, cats and dogs would burrow into that roof to keep warm. If it rained real hard, they'd come sliding out.

A brass monkey is a metal device used on ships during the early years of sailing. It held cannon balls ready for use in case of a naval attack. When it was really cold, freezing moisture would push the balls off, hence the saying.

A woman whom I did not know turned her chair around and said: "How about this one—did you know that the "ring around the rosie" poem is really a referral to the black plague that hit Europe?"

(I later looked this plague up. One-third of the population of Europe perished in that plague in and around 1347. It was properly called the bubonic plague, and was carried by rodents with fleas. The fleas then transmitted this plague to humans.)
"No. We don't know that one." She went on to explain it line by line.

"Ring around the rosie" refers to the round, red rash that forms on the skin when victims first contract the plague." We all quit drinking coffee and suddenly the circular sweet rolls in front of us didn't seem so appetizing.

She went on: "A pocket full of posies" refers to flowers that everyone carried in the belief that they would ward off the evil spirits that were killing everyone."

A young lady approached the table with a tray of what would have otherwise been some really good looking lemon bars. We all held our hands up as if we were warding off the very evil spirits of the plague ourselves.

As for the flowers, it occurred to me at that point that flowers at weddings way back then in the spring were mainly to cover up the smell of humans who hadn't bathed all winter. Furthermore, flowers at funerals were there for the same purpose, kind of, to cover up the smell of a body before embalming became popular. Maybe that was what the posies were really for back in 1347—covering up the smell of death. All this in church came to me, but I didn't bring it up. This lady was doing well enough on her own.

"Ashes, ashes," she went on to explain, referred to what was left after the diseased bodies were burned. The source to which I have since referred also speculated that "ashes, ashes" might have referred to the sneezing sound that people with the plague made, so if you got the ring around the rosie, and obviously the pocket full of posies didn't work, you went "a-choo, a-choo" which later turned into the sound made by the word "ashes."

Another possible explanation for this "ashes, ashes" was to the homes which were immediately burnt after the victims expired. Likely they were burned with the homes. Since everyone back then had a thatched roof, this part could have been pretty tricky.

Another explanation provided was that the term "ashes, ashes" referred to the blackish color of the victim's skin, which, since this was called the black plague, might make some sense.

"We all fall down" is almost self explanatory. With one out of three people succumbing to this disease, it must have seemed indeed like they were all falling down.

And now, the truth: First, no recorded version of this little children's song popped up until the early nineteenth century. For something to exist that long and not be written down is extremely unlikely. In fact, the first "plague" explanation of this rhyme popped up in the early 1900's, in a piece of written fiction. A parallel today exists in the book "The da Vinci Code," which purports to explain all sorts of weird connections between his painting and the bible.

The more likely explanation, according to research, is that the Protestant ban on dancing in the 19th century was gotten around by adolescents who came up with their "ring" dances, with sing-song rhymes. "Ashes, ashes" is a variation on "husha, husha," which refers to stopping the ring and becoming silent. The rest is pretty much self explanatory.

More coffee, anyone?

§

English: There's Absolutely No Getting Around It

There's absolutely no getting around it: I'm head over heels in love with, spend some time every day thinking about, couldn't live without, can hardly believe the depth of feeling I have-- for the English language.

You thought there was a woman involved, I bet'cha. Or a fast car, maybe red and low to the ground, so low that you could plow the snow off your driveway with it. Ah, rapture plus practicality–a sports car that would plow snow too. Nope.

You know, there's one thing about rapture–it's highly over rated. Rapture is a great word, though, no doubt about it. I'm in love with rapture. And I'm in love with the English language, at least, our American version of it.

I'll ride the English language to the end of the line. Right there, that "end of the line" thing, that's what's so rapturous about our language. We don't have to know the explicit words to express our feelings; we just have to know slang phrases and expressions that do it for us. Know where that "end of the line" expression came from? It came from railroading, specifically from the building of the rail lines that connected California to New York City back in the 1880's.

Imagine the difficulty of getting steel rail lines from the east coast, where they were manufactured, to California. They had to be sailed all the way down the Atlantic coast, around Cape Horn, which is the southernmost tip of Argentina–way down there at the bottom of South America--, then back up the west coast again. You think that went smoothly? I'll bet there were several hundred situations that took the wind right out of their sails, trying to do something like that. (Our rich vocabulary also owes a great deal to our nautical past, which is another completely different set of sayings, ones that talk about wind and sails and water.)

Then each rail had to be shipped to the end of the line, where ever the end of the line was that day. Do you have any idea how rough things were at the end of the line? They were so rough, you hardly had a Chinaman's chance in hell of getting there, much less getting rails there. Chinamen, who were looked down upon back then as worth even less than women, didn't have any chance. And now we have that saying: A Chinaman's chance in hell. If someone tells you that you don't have a Chinaman's chance in hell of doing whatever it is you're considering doing, you're about to get the wind knocked right out of your sails.

We and our language also got another saying from the end of the line: "hell on wheels.". Hell on wheels was at the end of the rail line. Hell on wheels was the description given to the accumulated collection of gamblers, Faro dealers, prostitutes, and other less savory characters that migrated to where the money was. Follow the money, that was what they did, to the end of the line. Where else did these young male workers have to spend their hard earned dollars? No where, because they were at the end of the line.

So when someone says, "That guy is hell on wheels," they're not talking about the way he drives, they're connecting him to the behavior generally seen only at the end of the line, where hell on wheels was.

When the end of the line moved on, which it did every month or so, hell moved with it, in wagons. On wheels.

If someone tells you that you don't have a Chinaman's chance in hell of doing something, then what you should do is make tracks out of there. Maybe on another day, you'll be riding the gravy train again. If you try to do it anyway, maybe you'll go to hell in a hand basket. That saying came from the hand-woven wicker baskets that the Chinamen slung from ropes down the cliffs of the Rockies. As they hung there, they hammered holes in the granite and packed them with black powder, hoping that the fuse was long enough and that someone pulled them up quickly enough. Hell in a hand basket. I guess so.

The Romans drove horse-drawn chariots that left ruts a certain width apart all over Europe. When better carriages were built, later on, they were of course built to fit the ruts that the Romans left in the roads. Building horse-drawn carriages became a major industry, so when railroad cars and locomotives were first built, the axles were of course built to the same size as the carriages, which were the same size as the Roman chariots.

When the United States built its railroads, well, I guess you know why our rails are the same distance apart as a Roman chariot. The next time you walk over a railroad track, remember another expression: When in Rome, do as the Romans do.

§

English: Hooker and Colonel

The English language is endlessly fascinating because of the origin of its words. Here are two I just came across. They both came from the Civil war.

Union General Joseph Hooker, an 1837 graduate of West Point, is credited with a successful reorganization of the Union cavalry, which was charged with the responsibility of "disrupting" Confederate General Robert E. Lee's supply line. The person put in charge of this first effort was Colonel Hugh Judson Kilpatrick.

Col. Kilpatrick returned from that first circular sweep through Dixie with every cow, pig, chicken, and bag of grain in their path, which allowed the Union army to advance far ahead of its supply line. This "foraging" will lead us directly to our first word.

General William T. Sherman, who became notorious as the instigator of "Sherman's Raiders," due to his order for the Cavalry—which he now commanded—to show South Carolina how he, Gen. Sherman, felt about them being the first to secede from the Union. "Let this march be one of the most horrible things in the history of the world." With that, his cavalry units, one of them headed by Kilpatrick, another of them headed by George Custer, tore through the countryside, leaving a path of destruction behind them.

"How shall I let you know where we are?" Kilpatrick once asked of Sherman. Sherman's replay: "Burn a town. We'll see the smoke." Kilpatrick's unit amongst all the cavalry units was without doubt the worst of them all at completely stripping the local population, including blacks, of everything of any value. They collected everything from silverware to silver buttons to fine dresses and bedding. A Union lieutenant wrote back to his wife: "Fine gold watches, silver pitchers, cups, spoons and forks are as common in our camp as blackberries. I have about a quart of rings, earrings, breastpins… for you and the girls."

General Sherman's personal take from the pillaging of South Carolina's towns and countryside was huge. The Union lieutenant above wrote: "Gen. Sherman has silver and gold enough to start a bank. His share of gold watches alone at just the sacking of Columbia, South Carolina, was 275." After all the valuables were collected, Columbia was burned to the ground.

(It isn't hard to see why the South hated the North for so long. One person described that all he saw after the Civil War ended was an endless number of brick chimneys extending up from piles of ashes.)

As to his part, Col. Custer was eventually relieved of his command because of his apparent inability to either follow orders or use basic military sense during battle.

The booty that the raiders collected each day was distributed to all the men in the command as follows. One-fifth, the finest choice, fell to the share of the commander and his staff, one-fifth to the field officers of the regiment, and three-fifths to the men of the company. This three-fifths was distributed by nightly auctions, where the soldiers bid on the items they wanted to buy. This "sale" was thus in the form of an auction, and was led by the commander of the regiment, who was always a colonel.

That explains why today's auctioneers still retain the honorary title of "colonel."

As to our next word, Union General Hooker, whom we mentioned first up above, may not have been anything above average as a military strategist, but morale in his unit was the highest of any unit, due to the number of women in his camp. He was renowned for his preference for liquor and ladies. "His headquarters," according on one historian, "was a place where no self-respecting man could go, and where no lady could go."

Col. Kilpatrick himself, perhaps inspired by Gen. Hooker's example, had audaciously brought two black women into his tent to serve, he said, as his "cooks." The camps buzzed with gossip about Col. Kilpatrick's sexual exploits with his cooks. Both Kilpatrick's and Hooker's camps soon attracted a substantial number of women of either ill repute, or southern women whose husbands had been killed in the war and whose homes had been burned to the ground. It must have seemed to these women that the only safe place left in the world was with these "conquerors."

So many women accumulated that they became known as Hooker's women. And that is where the term "hooker" came from.

Now you know.

§

Finnglish

The English language, about which I have written intensely, never fails to enchant me, especially up here on the northern end of the great rural American prairie. That's because, around here, you have to stay alert for Finnglish, which is a hybrid cross between English and Finnish that is heard quite often. (Less now. Those old timers have left us, and everyone else didn't get it that language like this is neat.)

Before those of you with Finnish roots gets his or her knickers bunched up about how the Finnish live in Finland and not here, yes. I know. Nonetheless, a good Finlander can live in either place. It is, after all, much easier to say "Finlander" than it is to say "someone of Finnish language-speaking origins." English is about easier, which is why all is welcome in this language.

On the other hand, speaking true "Finlander" isn't easy. So in case you visit around here and need to understand the spoken dialect, I've compiled a dictionary to help foreigners—anyone from some other town—understand the spoken words.

To truly speak Finlander, please remember that p's, b's, t's, and w's and v's can at random be used interchangeably, one for the other. Also, the first syllable of all Finnish words must be emphasized and drawn out and given great respect.

Here are some of the words I've learned:

Cawfiah: (caaaaaa-fiah) Local hot drink, used as a tranquilizer and mood leveler. To drink it properly, it must be first poured into a saucer. Then, the drinker must take one sugar cube and insert it in his or her mouth, through which the first swallow is filtered, after which the sugar cube is swallowed. Spilling is prohibited under the waste not want not proverb.

Furthermore, caaaaaaa-fiah is a lie serum in some locations, as in the local restaurant, where no one who consumes it can utter a whole truth, tranked to the gills as they are, usually. The good news is that everyone else is just as tranked, so no one cares about the truth.

Line: What cafiah often makes you do. Example: Ole is line now, and he's been line just about his entire life, especially when he drinks cafia.

Noose: Something just told to you that you didn't know a minute ago, probably by some one with whom you were drinking tranquilizers, as in, no noose is good noose.

Wetter: Also pronounced "wedder," and sometimes "weffer." Wedder is what's happening outside, meteorologically. For example, the wedder today is cloudy with a chance of rain, waitress, bring us another round of cafia.

Swatter: A machine used by Finlander farmers for putting hay and grain in a windrow. In other parts of the world, this is called a swather. It cannot be used when the wedder is raining, or during cafia breaks.

Wary: An adverb indicating an extreme something. For example, this cafia is wary good. Or, when it's forty below in the winter, the wedder is wary cold.

Bat: Opposite of good, as in, bat wedder.

Verse: To become more batter, as in, the wedder is verse now than it vas a while ago. Fooey!

Bret: Something from which you make a sannich.

Sannich: Two slices of bret. Makes a wery good sannich.

Budder: What you put on a sannich.

Letter: What your boots are made of.

Prick: A small building block made of hard clay. Since most small town's structures are built with these things, descriptions of buildings are often misinterpreted as character dispersions, and foreigners should avoid talking about them, lest the natives think you're talking about them. Let pricks be pricks, I always say.

I was in the hardware store one day and an elderly Finnish lady walked in, came up to me, and asked if I had any flatlights. She had quite a lisp on the "f" sound, I noticed, but I shook off the spray and led her over to a display of fluorescent lights that are flat and fasten up over the kitchen sink.

"No!" she strongly spat, and I was glad she was short. I took that blast pretty much in the chest, and led her over to the outdoor section, where some more flattish camping lamps were located.

"No!" once again she lisped, repeating the word "Flatlite! Flatlite!" Then she stomped out.

Someone else came in immediately after she left and asked me: "Did Sadie find a flashlight she was happy with?"

Oh. Um. No.

One should always learn the native language.

I looked at him and asked, "Cafia?"

And across the street to the restaurant we went.

§

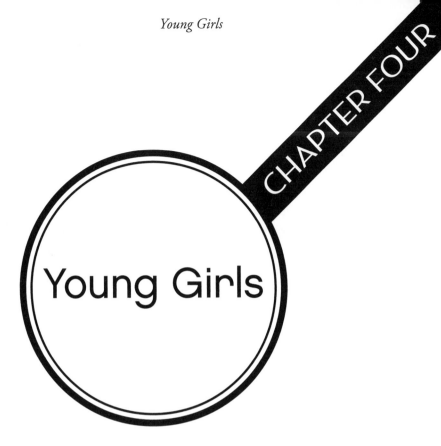

CHAPTER FOUR

Young Girls

Rituals

Throughout history, a great deal has been written about different cultures and their various rites of passage for males. "His-tory," that kind of explains that.

For instance in American Indian tribes, it was considered a test of your manly abilities to camp out in thick woods and shoot your first bear, then to go without food until you were dizzy and had strange dreams. Maybe then they'd let you hang up in the air by ropes attached to wooden splinters fastened through your chest muscles.

That was nothing. The rites of passage that are required of today's society of The Tribe of Girls are far worse than bad dreams and hanging by your chest hairs.

Years ago, I decided to dedicate the rest of my life to getting intimately acquainted with a Tribe of Girls. To do that, I gained the trust of one of them by wining and dining several of them, and sending them flowers and chocolates. None of them trusted me. It took me a long time to find one that did. The Girls of the Tribe are smart, and I think that They were onto me. It took me a long time to find one that wasn't.

Except in retrospect, it only now is occurring to me that She probably was, and I didn't know it.

Back when this all started, there were grants to study wolves. There were none for studying Tribes of Girls. I thought that was because no one was interested. Time has shown me that there was interest, but studying wolves just seemed safer. Had I stuck with studying wolves, I'd have saved a bunch of money on flowers and candy. Plus, a couple of chunks of red meat would have been cheaper than all those dinners I paid for.

It did take me a long time to find the Female; it took thirty years, matter of fact. There were a lot of Girls out there to check out, and it was slow work, because the Female of the species is pretty suspicious, I'll tell you. Finally, I managed to grab onto one of the apparently well-qualified Females available, and marry her before she got away.

I had to wine her. I had to dine her, and give her pretty words and flowers, until she seemed to like me. I hoped, through her, to study the rest of The Tribe of Girls.

I set out to trap her, and soon found myself trapped instead. One day I was a scientist studying them, and the next, I was helplessly held in a spell-trap she had placed on me, confined to her tipi.

Several years went by, during which I believe I was under the influence of drugs, which she laced the food she gave me with. When she was done with me, which I know she was because suddenly her cooking went south, I awoke and found that I was surrounded by my own Tribe of Girls--The Old Girl, and three Young Girls. She had drugged me and used me to start her own Tribe of Girls. This was one formidable creature. I never saw it coming.

In the tipi in which they confine me, time has taught me that truly understanding them is proving to be far more difficult than I had earlier estimated. Although I have gained their trust to the point at which I am allowed to watch some of their minor ceremonies and unique ordeals and tests, I'm pretty much out of it.

Some of their rites I have actually observed, some I can only speculate about. I see daily evidence of their secret goings-on, and must infer behavior traits from that evidence. I have, for instance, been vehemently denied any participation in something called "Searching for a Training Brah." They also go on frequent "Lingerie Hunts." They all return from that one totally exhausted. Of course, anyone would, since this hunt occurs in a particularly vicious place called a "Maul."

It's been seventeen years of my cautiously letting them get to know me, and finally, the other day, my Tribe of Girls gave me one of my greatest thrills by lowering their guard and letting me observe—"Remember, you cannot utter on single, solitary word!"—a ritual called the "Merry Khay Makeover."

It was awful. I don't know how they could endure it. First, a medicine woman from some other Tribe came with a huge container of secret tools and herbs. Then they all sat at the kitchen table and pulled their long hair back and fastened it by driving steel pins into their scalp. That, judging by their grimaces, must have truly hurt.

After a prolonged period of pinching and squeezing each other's faces with wooden sticks and bristly brushes, they went at each other's eyes with black mud and metal pinchers. All during this procedure, they complained stoically about why Tribes of Girls all have to go through this torture.

Next, no doubt to staunch the bleeding, they plastered a mask made of some kind of magic white clay all over their faces, leaving only their eyes peering helplessly out. As the mask dried and turned into concrete, there was a lot of groaning and more than once, one of them asked: "When in Hell is this stuff coming off?" As the concrete dried and shrank, it pulled their lips into a sneering smile. They could hardly talk.

They laughed a lot while all this was going on, to show their bravery while enduring this agony. They are indeed a brave Tribe.

When the shrinking concrete had nearly pulled their lips right off their faces, they peeled a bit of the concrete mask up at the edge, and yanked the whole thing off, yelping with pain. Then they put different colors of magic clay on their eyes and cheeks and lips. Some of the clay was blue; some was red. I'd guess it was concocted of berries and herbs. I can only guess, because they wouldn't tell me. When I asked, they pretended like they didn't know. Even the visiting medicine woman clammed right up and became very evasive about the clay's origins. It must be some powerful stuff.

Some of the colors were so garish and so horribly indescribable that I could only guess they put it on to scare away the demons that force Tribes of Girls to put themselves through this rite of passage. They must be scary demons. I was scared. I found it extremely upsetting the way they spread this stuff all over themselves.

Just when I though they were finished, they started poking themselves in the eyes again.

I secretly observed all this for about an hour. When they started talking about removing the hairs from their legs, I lost my appetite for any further research, and I left.

I should have studied a wolf pack.

§

Pulling 15's Leg

Children grow up. We spend the first several years of their lives in a hurry for them to act their age, and the next several years regretting it. As they grow up, one of the problems of parenting is putting enough tension on the rope to hold them in the nest and out of harm's way, yet letting enough slack in the rope to let them find their wings with a minimum of danger.

15, our oldest daughter, had been out with her girlfriends the night before, one of whom—this is where the "slack" part comes—had her driver's license. They went to a movie and were home quite early, so her mother and I, who were basking in the post-traumatic complacency of a fledgling's first successful flight, were suddenly alarmed the next day at the dinner table to hear the following tale unfold.

I'm telling it so that those of you now with similar-aged children may be warned. Perhaps this telling will help you avoid what we had to go through. For those parents for whom this is too late, I extend the shared sympathy of mutual experience, the empathy of overall understanding, and the frustration of knowing that you have very little hope of controlling what happens to your kids once they're out of the nest.

In other words, good luck.

15 said that after the movie, they drove around town a little, saw some kids they knew, waved and hollered, drove some more, and so forth. Since the only place in town open at that time of night was a combination convenience store-gas station, they decided to stop and check it out.

Inside the brightly-lit apparent safety of the quick stop, they all three got Mountain Dews from the large glass cooler. On the way to the checkout counter up front, they dawdled and giggled over various items for sale on the counters. They were having fun, my daughter said. They were, in other words, enjoying their freedom.

An older lady came up to 15, 15 said to us. And how old is this "older" lady, I asked 15, wishing to get ahead of this unfolding drama.

She told us that her hair was about half grey, anyway, the lady came up, and said: "You look just like my daughter. I miss her so; she died of cancer last year after an awful time in the hospital."

The lady, 15 said, seemed so nice but so sad that what could she do but listen. Her girlfriends had moved away to the counter up front, leaving her alone with this woman. The woman continued to pour out her somber story.

As this story came out, my mind leaped ahead to discover all the ways a total stranger could take advantage of a teenager on her first night out alone in the world. I kept a calm look on my face. Kept my trembling hands beneath the table.

I could picture any young woman listening politely, as they had been taught, to an adult. What danger could they suspect?

After a bit more of the story, the lady said to 15: "You have been very kind to listen to me. Would you do one thing for me?" Right here, I wanted to leap to my feet and do something. But what? Apparently no one is safe here on the northern end of the prairie anymore, when things like this can happen.

15 said, yes, sure, what can I do for you?

The lady said, "It would mean so much to me if my daughter had had the chance to say goodbye to me. As I go out the door, would you wave at me and say, "Goodbye, mom?"

Sure, said 15. As the lady went out past the checkout counter, she said something to the clerk, turned around, and waved.

15, in a voice loud enough to be heard, said, "Goodbye, Mom." The lady waved again, and left. Suddenly, 15 said, the three of them weren't having that much fun in there anymore, so they went to the cashier to pay for their stuff, but when 15's turn to pay came, the cashier said, "What about your mother's gas?"

15 said, oh, she's not my mother, and realized how lame that sounded.

The cashier said, "Very funny, that'll be $40.00."

Through the window, 15 saw the lady just reaching for her car door, and said that she cannot remember anything except sprinting out the door, running for that car, scattering people left and right.

At this point, having listened intently, 15's mother looked upon the verge of having a heart attack. Enough said.

To myself, I thought: Oh, no. Con artists are mostly harmless until you corner them. What was my daughter thinking? I'm a failure as a parent. Why didn't I warn her about stuff like...

15 continued. "Stop! Wait!" she shouted as she raced for the lady, who, when she

saw 15 coming, hurried a bit too much and fumbled just enough with the door latch to slow her entry into her car.

"Stop!" 15 shouted again, as she ran. The lady was all in except for her leg.

15 said she couldn't think of anything else to do but grab the lady's leg in a bear hug and begin pulling on it.

Just like I'm pulling yours.

Just like she pulled ours.

§

Girls: Moons

Much ado has been made throughout time about the monthly cycles of the moon, and about the monthly cycles of women. Ado. Now, there's a word.

Forget the moon. I don't live with the moon. Instead, my ado has to do with the monthly cycles of women. There's a lot of ado there, piles and piles. It's above average ado in most aspects, size-wise.

Ado about women has little to do with science, especially the science that I, The Prairie Spy, can bring into crisp, clear focus. That's my job. Scientific observation.

I can take or leave the moon, because I don't live with four moons. Instead, I live with Four Girls, all of whom have reached that particular biological age wherein they manifest certain…ahem…similarities of physical and mental behavior with one another, and with the moon. Ahem, ahem, ahem.

To be sure, a lot of this PMS behavior that is attributable to monthly hydraulic hormone surges in the human female has actually, it seems to me, to have been there since birth, waiting for an excuse—any excuse—to have the floodgates opened, and the torrents loosed.

The torrents are loose around here a lot, and that's a scientific fact. Young Girls practice as much as possible when they're little, so they'll be ready when their hormones are. Open up those gates. Stand back.

When the monthly flood of ado becomes so torrential around here that it threatens to drown me, I lower my eyes. (Rule 1: Hope they don't notice you.) and repeat to myself these words: "They love me, in their own Girl Tribal Way; I am their Earth, their reason for being, the center of their orbital path. They are my Four Moons. They are here, captured in their heavenly orbits by my irresistible gravitational force. (I learned all this from another Guy named Copernicus. He evidently lived with Girls also.)

Let's be clear here (which would be a first), we're talking in metaphorical similes here. I don't have much gravitational mass…although perhaps there is a certain magnetic something…

Back to the moons. When they're all "orbiting" together, I like that the best. It's fun being an Earth for them then. They (The Girls, in case you're confused) hug and kiss and sing and giggle and have lots of fun. Sometimes, they even shine on me, sort of. But just as the earth's moon affects the earth's tides, the Girl-Moons affect mine, and when their monthly orbits deteriorate and reach glandular disintegration, one can do nothing right. All you can do is avoid eye contact. Like when they all came home the other evening from Sha-Ping (A weird Tribal Custom) in town together:

"All right! Who tracked in all this mud? And what in (Tribal Word, can't repeat it here) is that piece of junk stinking up the kitchen sink!"

I don't know about the mud, Darling Tribal Chief Girl, you know I'd never do that, but that's my tractor carburetor there in the sink, soaking in NAPA's world-famous carb cleaner. It had kind of a miss around 1200 rpms, so I…

"Dad! Eeeeuuuwww! What are you doing to mom's sink?"

Well, like I said, that low-speed idle jet was kind of plugged so….

"Whoa! That's a major bogus smell you got going there, dad. Chad's supposed to pick me up in an hour. Now, thanks to you, I'll smell like a racetrack!"

Maybe your boyfriend needs a lesson in carburetor overhaul. You know, I could help him…

"Have you lost your mind? In the kitchen sink?"

I don't think….

"Who took my Oreo cookies that I've been saving for when I'm desperate? I need them! I crave them! Chocolate! Now! Who did it? I'll rip out their heart, I'll…"

"Ooooooh no! We're out of Ibuprofen again. That's the third bottle this month. Oooohhh no!"

Listen, Girls, have you forgotten that I'm your central orbital reason for being? Your earth, your….

"Give it a rest, Dad. Some of us have got some major problems going here. We've all got stomach cramps beyond reality. And headaches you wouldn't believe. Nausea. You."

Must be the flu that's going around.

"Get real, Dad."

"Yeah, Dad."

"Whatever, Dad!"

"You'll have to fix supper again tonight, dear. Check the laundry pile, while you're at it. We're all indisposed."

Yes, Moon….I mean, dear.

§

Girls: Twits, Flat as the Walls

"Hello. My sisters are all morons," said 12 matter-of-factly. The phone had rang and she had gotten there first, knowing it was likely some boy. These days, it's a race for the phone. Boys call on the phone. The phone belongs to the quick and the cute. Her, of course.

12 may be last in arrival, but she is infinitely more motivated and amply capable of reminding the entire world—especially 14 and 16, her first-but-not-most sisters—that she is not least. Last but not least. A scientifically supportable theory around here.

14 and 16 can take care of themselves, so don't be concerned. They are each the valiant and proud survivors of countless duels to the split end with electric blow dryers. Most duels in the Tribe of Girls, however, do not involve any weapons other than The Sharp Tongue, an ancestrally inherited trait bequeathed down through centuries of customs, ceremonies, and continual sharpening during exchanges of wit.

From the time the first Neanderthal Man left his underwear lying used side up on the floor of the cave, Girls have verbally slashed and parried their way up to Cave and/or Teepee Queen, by saying sharply to their male:

"Ooooggg! Ahhhhdmmmmmsssttt! Ugh! Aarrrgggaaahhh! And oh yes, ggggrrr ssccaaaieeedddooo!"

(Interpreted, this means 'pick'um up right now, Sweet Cheeks, or you'll pay Dear-Lee.')

Dear-Lee, I now know, is an ancient God called often upon around here. It didn't take long to figure out that if you mess with Her, you mess with your destiny.

And your supper.

All this savage teepee repartee is new to me, I have come to realize as I enter the latest outbursts into the journal I keep for research. I was a brother. Not a sister. All this is completely foreign to me, so I'm keeping notes. Growing up as a brother, one's primary purpose in life was to practice upon one another the art of maiming, chopping, and hitting—all necessary skills to provide and defend a teepee against outside enemies.

Where little girls try to verbally twit one another into submission, little boys quickly learn that striking is quicker. We learn not to bring fewer weapons to the fray than the other boy has got. Sticks and stones and so forth. Hit'em in the eye.

Here in the teepee, every word uttered is a twit in some sister's eye.

"Where'd you get that lipstick? At the undertaker's?"

"Your hair looks so…so…soo nerdy!"

"Hey, doorknob! Take a pill!"

"The Tell-A-Phone's for you! I think it's Death-Breath!"

Now I know why it has become customary for the father to give away the bride. Plus throw in some money to boot. Maybe a couple of goats and a cow. And lots of wine.

Giving away the daughter as a bride is less of a give-away than it is a hand-off of a ticking bomb, in this case a bomb emitting twitting sounds. "Here," the father of the bride is saying, "you charge into the pack with this one for a while." It's like playing quarterback with the Viking football team, knowing you're going to take a beating. Here's some money to buy bandages, here's some goats to symbolize your new role in life, and here's some booze to numb you up.

The other day I overheard the ultimate Tribe of Girls insult, an age-old twit meant not for the male ear, the ultimate major all-time super-twit of the ages, in existence as far back as there have been monkeys capable of pantomiming this message:

"YOU'RE SO FLAT EVEN THE WALLS ARE JEALOUS!"

That is the Mother of all twits, and I, The Prairie Spy and official researcher of The Guy's Club, was unfortunate enough to overhear it, and record it for posterity.

"My sisters are both so ugly they can't come to the phone," 12 said into the telephone receiver, right after she answered it with the moron informational.

"Well," she said to me upon receiving my aggrieved parental look, and giving me her superior opinion back: "They are such losers!"

Last but not least.

§

Clothing War

We're into teenage daughters, clothes and cars in an overpowering way at my house. Just-turned-16, as she moves about the house and through her chores, assumes a pace that only a mother turtle could love. But let someone be looking out the window and say: "Look at that hot car!" Then, hormones flush her cheeks, adrenaline floods her muscles, her legs turn into rockets, and she streaks over to the window where she says: "Hey! Check it out, man!"

"Totally unreal!" So says 14, her eyes cool.

Yet the third and youngest sister has her say. She's 12: "Oooooo. He's cute." (At 12? Ahhhh please no.)

14 says: "Get a life. Men are pigs!" I like 14. A dad could stay sane an extra-long time with a daughter who holds firm to that thinking.

Somebody, along in here, usually pipes in with: "CHILL OUT!" or some such teenspeak. The "total" car has passed on by, and they have only each other once again. For those of you who either don't know, or have forgotten, or have a well-developed case of protective amnesia, sisters are sometimes unthrilled with each other. For about 23 hours a day.

Each of them is convinced that they were individually placed upon this earth in this particular household with this dismaying set of sister-things—there are three sisters in this house—for the express purpose of wearing as many of the others' favorite pieces of clothing as is humanly possible. Mornings around here come like a combination fashion show and the trading pit of the wall street stock exchange.

Sisters come up out of the basement laundry room, waving articles of clothing before them like Vikings used to wave battle shields. When this happens, almost always the waver is upset, and is shrieking something like: "Whoworethisandleftitinthemiddleofthefloorandiwantedtowearitnowican't…..!!!!!"

There's more. You get the idea. Pure anguish, teenage style.

Sometimes, though, the waver comes up the stairs wearing subservience like a serf before her queen. When that happens, they're also waving clothing, but this time they're waving it more as a flag of truce than as a flag of battle. Ah, yes. They've come to parley a trade, and that requires an entirely different personality front. Instead of confrontation and exclamation, they're into charm and cunning.

At these moments, I swear there's a con man running a flim-flam school in the basement, that's how good these Young Girls can be.

"Whose is this?" the waver will peep in her most meek and humble fashion, holding up an article of clothing.

No one even turns around to look. The response to a question this dumb is always one and only one thing. Without even seeing which item of clothing is in question, the Other Two always say: "Mine!" "Mine!" "No way!" "It's mine!" "I wore it last!" (As if that really matters, but it's becoming readily apparent that possession truly is nine tenths of the law.)

The waver then must reveal part of her poker hand, but, not tooooo much. After all, she's already acting like she likes these fellow sister-things. Enough is enough, usually, with that. But this morning, she opens with the slave gambit: "I'll wash dishes on your day if I can wear this to the dance-school-town-etc."

And then hard ball begins.

"Yeah? You still haven't washed the dishes for the time I let you wear my best stockings." Then comes the beggars stock reply:

"Really! What makes you think they were yours. Mom said I could wear them." Good counter.

The psychology of this manner of interaction escapes me. I'm not certain I understand it. But it's good. Very good.

With the patience of one to the trading pit born, the sister-thing owning the clothing item replies, with the poker face of a river boat gambler: "When did you ever ask Mom? Let's go ask her." And then she makes a great fake at going to ask Mom.

Mom's in the other room. She has a headache. The first person who asks her anything will return missing her head clear down to the ankles.

Not knowing that Mom is indisposed, the sister-waver on the stairs falters, and her battle is lost.

For today.

§

Prom Night

This goes back, way back, to an autumn day when, as if to remind me that life wasn't already whizzing by at light speed, there came into the farmyard a long black limousine. It stopped and lurked right outside the front door of the house. Right there in front of our door. Big black limos with shiny blacked-out windows don't occupy normal space—they lurk.

I looked at it from where I stood, leaning on the shovel with which I had been planting an apple tree, a shovel which now served to steady me. The tinted darkness of the limo's windows was ominous in that its occupants could see out, but you could not see in.

I knew why it was there, there other than to remind me that time is not within our control. It was prom night—the limousine was here to scoop up two of The Young Girls, the limo being the twenty-first century's equivalent of a pumpkin drawn by a team of mice turned into horses, carrying children turning into adults, away to a dance. What made all this so emotional was that, this time, the pumpkin was carrying away two of my children. There was no escape. They too were growing up.

I had a sudden memory of The Young Girls as Little Girls who, on a warm summer day, covered with mud, one still in a mud-soaked sagging diaper, stopped playing long enough to pose for the camera. Stopped making mud castles and pies with spoons and spatulas and dishes.

Right there in the driveway where the limo lurked.

Then I remembered them a little older, with the coaster wagon tied haphazardly to Sally, the Black Lab, whose body English served to remind everyone around her that she—not these usurpers—was our first child. She wouldn't pull that wagon though, no sir, which didn't seem to matter to the Little Girls. Regardless of Sally's attitude, they spent blissful hours dressing her up and tying her up and what all, while she just stood there, patiently waiting for their attention to shift elsewhere. She stood and endured.

Right there in the driveway where the limo lurked.

The next memory is of The Young Girls, older still, and it is snowing, a warm snow, wet and sticky and great for making snow sculptures. The Young Girls at that age brought to snow art a new attention to detail that was amazing. The figures that they created, with hats and gloves and arms, stood for weeks, and reminded me each day when I left for work that children gain new skills, and grow older, even though the snow people seemed to stand there unchanged. I say "seemed." After a few days, the snowmen began to show how time, for them too, was passing quickly. It does that for snowmen, and for children. They both grow old.

Right there in the driveway where the limo lurked.

Suddenly, a door in the black limo opened and Young Men appeared, all dressed up, holding their offering of flowers. They wore grown-up tuxes, with sharp pleats in their pants, and patent leather shoes that caught the late day sun, and brilliant smiles..

I looked, and my hands had abandoned the shovel for a camera, with which I somewhat automatically begin taking pictures of young excitement, and anticipation, and shy looks, and jerky moves, as The Young Men posed self consciously with The Young Girls. Then they were clumsily pinning corsages on, and the results are crooked, and everyone is smiling at everyone else, even though the smiles look frozen, and somewhat manufactured. Is this fun, the smiles seemed to ask? They all seemed a little bit confused about what fun is, and is this exactly what each of them is supposed to be doing, in this ritual in front of the magic pumpkin in which they arrived moments ago.

They probably think that we, The Old Girl and I, being adults, know what they should be doing, and they likely wish they could do it. At least then, someone would be happy. We are, by our presence, the unwitting source of a great deal of their awkwardness. Getting the hell out of there will solve that dilemma, though, so they bundle their sharp pleats and shiny dresses and patent leather pumps into the pumpkin and speed out of there, all black windows and motion and leaving, taking both the proof of our existence—and our measure of time passing—away with them.

We stand there, and watch them go, and think about children playing in the mud, and a black dog tied to a wagon, and snow men, and our own fading mortality.

In the Lamaze method book, I don't remember any of this being covered.

§

Spilled Chickens

(This column goes back to when the oldest Young Girl was 17. It's one of my favorites.)

It was an otherwise ordinary day. Me? I was just home from work, sitting at my ordinary kitchen table, enjoying the ordinary end of what was an ordinary—hallelujah!—day.

Plainly, everything was ordinary. It was in that condition that we often lament as boring. Boring is nothing but boring up to that point when ordinariness is violently ripped asunder by the Extraordinary. The calm surface of everything is suddenly all splooshed up like someone just threw in a boulder. The splash soaks you to the bone.

At that point, you find yourself sitting there, dripping, thinking about how plain and boring life was just a moment ago, and about how you kind of thought it was maybe too boring. Now? Now, you're looking for a towel, and the kind you need hasn't ever been sold at retail.

Seventeen (The Young Girls are identified, if you remember, by their respective ages. There's 13—going on 24—15—going on 24—and 17—also going on 24. Seventeen just walked in the front door. She had just returned in the much-fancied Little Red Car that, she claims, calls her name at night and begs her to drive hither and yon about the countryside, a tank and a half a night.

Seventeen came in and said: "Dad, don't be mad. I have to tell you something…"

I looked up from the plain and ordinary book which I had been reading, assumed the most ordinary look I could muster, and shouted: "YOU'RE NOT PREGNANT, ARE YOU?"

"Dad! I'm only 17. Quit that."

I guess, then that everything else you're going to tell me is, by comparison, pretty, ummm, ordinary, huh?

"I didn't hurt The Red Car, and it really wasn't my fault," continued 17. Different expressions were trading places on her face. Truth seemed to be wrestling accountability there, and her face was showing the strain of serving as the mat for the match.

"Difficult as this is to explain, dad, well, you know…well, The Car just ran into 47 frozen chickens and a turkey," said 17, quite, I thought, straight faced. Plainly, I thought to myself, this will not be an ordinary story. Yippee.

Where did this close encounter between you and the world's proven reserve of cold poultry take place?

"There was ice and I was just starting The Little Red Car and it wasn't my fault and it was in neutral cause it won't start in gear and it kinda did it by itself." The Great

Wrestling Match was now using her hands, which seemed to believe that large amounts of waving were directly correlatable to large amounts of innocence in this affair.

You…..you hit 47 frozen chickens?

"And a turkey," she added. (I didn't want this to ever end. Even now, I was thinking column. Great column.) These chickens, I asked, were they crossing the street and got caught in a sudden temperature drop? Has the warming of the planet reversed and gone a-fowl, suddenly? (Wait, I thought to myself, until Al Gore hears this.)

"It didn't hardly dent it," she said in a whisper.

Dent what, I asked, suspecting the hard part was coming.

"Dent mom's new freezer." She added, "in the garage."

Ah, the freezer in the garage. (The ice thickens.) I better go look, huh?

Out in the plain ordinary garage, I switched on the lights, and winced. Mr. Gibson the Freezer looked like he'd just been whopped in the stomach by Mohammed Ali, and had not yet had the sense to fall down. He was standing there crouched over his belly, held up by the back wall of the garage, against which he had been crushed into a vee. The chicken packages strung out in front of him looked like he had vomited them out pretty hard.

I went over to him, touched him. I couldn't believe it: he was still running. Does it hurt, I asked him?

"Real bad," he gasped, as frozen chicken giblets oozed out of him.

"Tell…" he had to catch his breath. "Tell Lady Kenmore the Dryer goodbye for me."

OK, I told him, hang on. I'll help you.

Then he said: "Get these chickens off my back, they…" and with that Mr. Gibson the Freezer expired.

My friend the freezer was gone. And I, survivor guilt written all over me, was left to break the news to The Old Girl, who was going to be unhappy. She was going to be upset.

And when she's upset, …..

This used to be such a plain ordinary day.

§

Little Red Car

There's a lonely little red car sitting in our driveway this early fall morning. The dew that condenses and runs down the front of its headlights leaves a trail behind it, much the same as tears might.

It's crying this morning because we took 18 off to college yesterday, where cars aren't really wanted, and because 16, the heir apparent, doesn't love anything with a stick shift.

I never thought I'd see the day when I'd mourn a car sitting idle on a driveway where the dust hadn't completely settled in two years, but I was. After 18 got her license, home became a pit stop, and we kind of became her pit crew.

Leaving 18 at school provided me with some images that linger. One was seeing three sisters locked together in a group hug for the first time. The last time they were that close, they were fighting over a blouse that each of them desperately wanted.

Or, they fought over the telephone. Or someone's favorite socks. They actually got close to one another many times, now that I think back on it. These moments of closeness were accompanied by appropriate language, such as:

"You give that back to me, you twerp!"

"No way, Hozay!"

"Way! Way! Way!"

"Who died and made you queen for a day, huh?"

And so forth. I had suspected all along that they actually liked each other, but the real image of them walking back from the dorm, arms around one another—well, that helped.

14 and 16 are taking their sister's absence remarkably well. Let's listen in on them:

"16: "You sneak! What were you doing in 18's room, huh?"

14: "Nothing! What were you doing outside her door?"

16: "Checking to make sure you didn't take...YOU DID! YOU DID! I GET THAT! SHE SAID I COULD HAVE THAT!"

14: "PROVE IT. TRY!"

Ah yes, it's been said before, but I'll say it again. Today's teenagers adjust to change quickly.

I went outside to see Red Beretta, the abandoned auto.

Well, I said to Red: Red, you look as lonely as I feel, with 18 gone.

Red didn't move, just said: "Trade me. I can still play the game."

What do you mean, trade you?

"This team sure doesn't need me. Look, this is a simple game. She clutches, she shifts, you put gas in me, I get her back home safely." I could swear I heard a muffled sob when he said "home."

16 will learn to love you, you'll see.

"No she won't. She hates me. She thinks my clutch pedal is the brake half the time. The other half of the time, she slips the clutch and makes my insides hurt. This is a sport, with precise skills. 18 could synchronize a shift with the best of them. You should know. You taught her. You could drive me, but all you do is work…"

OK, OK, I get the point, but she'll be back in a few weeks, and she…

Red sputtered out a couple half-hearted ticks and said, "Uh, uh. You bench me and I'll rust up so fast I swear you'll hear fenders falling off me in the middle of the night."

So where do you want to go?

Red snorted and said, "That's easy. I've never been to college before. 18 and me are a team." He shifted gears kind of, and said, in a sadder, quieter voice, "I know you miss her too. Those tears you thought you saw earlier, they weren't mine. Cars can't cry." He coughed, went on: "How about we do the best we can for a little while, and see what happens. I guess we're all a team, kind of."

That sounds pretty sensible.

"One other thing," Red said, "I feel empty."

Hey, I'll get some gasoline…

"Not that kind of empty, you know?"

Yeah. I know.

§

GaGa

Boobs are in the news lately.

It's about time. For two reasons, at least.

One of the rather noteworthy aspects of boobs is really only noteworthy because our society has made it noteworthy, namely, that they shouldn't be acknowledged as in existence at all. Cleavage then becomes noteworthy as well, when and if it should be demonstrated.

The existence of cleavage? Gasp! She's showing cleavage? OMG! Gasp! That must mean she has breasts! Which must mean she's loose. Now, I don't mean loose as in the loose that caused Howard Hughes to design and build the first uplifting apparatus so that Jane Russell in the movie "The Outlaw," had her rather generous assets pushed right into the face of a society that itself frowned on such demonstrations of human anatomy. Because of that push, MGM at first refused to print the picture. Howard Hughes hired a slew of telephone dialers to call every minister in the country protesting this possible lewd behavior by Hollywood. The ensuing uproar guaranteed "The Outlaw" immediate success.

Not that kind of loose. No. I mean loose as in morally loose. Women are somewhat both fortunate and unfortunate in their having these things. Fortunate in that society's dictates regarding admitting that they have them means they can attract extra attention by wearing clothing that hints at their existence. As in "GASP!"

They are unfortunate when it comes to size, which brings to existence the continual unspoken competition that large versus small seems to initiate amongst them. At a time when breast implants are still the best part of $5000.00, some women still consider this a small price to pay for large boobs.

Let's see how one woman has taken advantage of the first of these "unfortunate" scenarios: the "extra attention" scenario. To do this, we're going to focus on a young woman named Lady GaGa, who is becoming well known in the electronica pop field of rock and roll, both for her music, which I read is quite danceable, and for her, well, for her two other reasons.

A recent picture of her in last week's issue of Newsweek showed her in one of her more creative costumes. I don't know a lot about her, but I do know that her selection of the name "GaGa" didn't come because of her music. Her music is ok, but it's still created with typical instrumentation and vocals.

It's her costumes that are attracting her the extra attention that performing artists seem to need to break free of their peer group and achieve stardom. Her music is fairly creative; her voice is ok; her costumes, though, they truly are something.

First, a couple of definitions are in order. "Gaga," according to various dictionaries, is derived from the French language, and means foolish, or crazy. In modern usage, it has come to mean dazzling, as in "marked by wild enthusiasm." Without a doubt, Lady GaGa's costumes are all of those definitions, and more.

Now let's define the word "nipple," and for those of you who already kind of see where this is going, congratulations. Sometimes I don't even know that. According to various dictionaries again, the word "nipple" derives from Old English usage, from the word "neb," which back a thousand years meant birds beak, or various other things that protruded outward. It has been used to describe mountain peaks, also.

A letter written to Newsweek the next week after the Lady GaGa article, said, more or less: "As a mother of a 14-year-old boy, I cannot believe you published a picture of Lady GaGa that showed her nipple." She went on to huff and puff about how pictures like this are going to ruin her son, and other sons, and huff, huff, huff, puff, puff, puff, etc.

I, immediately upon reading that letter, went off and found last week's Newsweek and a magnifying lens, and Eureka! There indeed, after intense scrutiny, I found that I myself have unfortunately too been placed on the road to moral ruin.
I tell you. I had no idea that breasts had nipples. Small protuberances, whatever. I am shocked. Shocked, I tell you.

To the mother: I've got bad news for you: If by the age of 14, your son doesn't know that breasts exist, you've got other, larger issues that you're going to have to deal with. Either you've had him locked up in a closet for the past few years, or he himself is in there voluntarily. Maybe you're in there. It could be time for one of you to come out.

So, there she was, Lady "Dazzle," a mature young woman, demonstrating to all the shocked world that she has breasts. Not only that, that those breasts have nipples.

The fact that something so common can get her national newsworthiness would seem to demonstrate that it's not Lady GaGa that's gaga.

It's us.

§

Grandkids, Eleven's Lesson

It has been my greatest duty and pleasure this summer, since my daughter, her husband, and their now-11-month-old infant have tarried here on their way to bigger and better things, to teach Eleven as many necessary skills as possible.

Like climbing the stairs.

"That's it," I encouraged Eleven, after checking to see that her mother was safely out of sight and sound, "just scooooooooch your knee up on that next step, thaaaaaat's it, now briiiiiingggg that other fat little leg up to the step—DON'T LOOK DOWN!!!—oookaay, now focus, Eleven, briiiing that other knee up to the next step—NO DON'T EAT THAT PIECE OF GARBAGE YOU JUST PICKED UP OFF THE STEP!!!—let's get back to the neeeeexxxt step, you've got it oh you're sooooo talented I'll bet you'll be in the Olympic gymnastic tryouts any day now put your knee up on that next step thaaaaaaat's it—OOOPS YES THE KITTY THINKS YOU SHOULD STAND UP ON THE STEP AND WAVE AT HER DON'T DO THAT!!!—much better."

And so forth. It's a long way up the stairs when you're eleven months old. I know. You're saying what kind of a grandpa would teach a kid that young to climb the stairs but my logic here is sound as a rock. Anyone who thinks some kid isn't going to make for the stairs as soon as your back is turned lives in a dream world.

Besides, climbing them isn't the real problem, just like taking off in an airplane isn't the real problem either, it's getting your butt back on the ground in some reasonable facsimile of what it left in that's at issue.

"OKAY NOW PAY ATTENTION and we're going to work on our descent next, Eleven. Scooch your butt on over to the edge of that top step like this, no, not exactly like that, more like this," and I kind of went first for an example but I'd forgotten how small those steps were in this old country house built back when stairs more closely resembled Jacob's ladder to heaven and I slid five or six before I got everything under control.

Eleven sat on the top step clapping and laughing and generally not paying attention to that old saying: "There are old pilots and bold pilots but there are no old bold pilots." This was going to be more of a challenge than I had first thought, and now my butt hurt.

"There you go," I told her as I slid her off the first step, "get your foot down to this nexxxxxxxt one juuuuuust like that oh you're good now don't look for the kitty just put the other foot dooooooown liiiike that on you've got it NO DON'T GRAB FOR THE RAILING IT'S TOO HIGH UP!!! that's it now eeeeeassyy just get to the edge of the next one no give grandpa back his glasses he needs them more than you do NO DON'T THROW THEM OVER THE BANNISTER oh heck that's alright they're just drugstore specials anyway oh don't cry if you cry you'll get the stair steps all slick and then you'll have a big problem."

About now, I began to remember teaching my kids to drive a car. I bought an old straight stick, cut off the roof, and turned them loose in the hay field with several bales of hay for pretend traffic.

I resisted the immediate urge to build a set of training stairs out of bales of hay, and went back to what I had.

"Okay now you're on your own, Eleven, let's see you put that fat little leg down like I showed you oooohhh that's it you're on your own you've got it you've got it you're going to be the champion stair butt slider of all times NO DON'T LOOK UP NEVER LOOK UP YOU'LL GET DIZZY okay that's better now one more just one more step oh you've got it you've got it."

We were down two stair steps and I had to pee but duty required finishing what we'd started here overactive prostate thingy be darned we'll just ignore that for a while. (One could not completely eliminate the possibility that grandpa would be in diapers about the time Eleven gets out of them.)

"Ready, Eleven? Here we go one more step don't worry you should have seen your mom trying to sneak up these steps when she came home real late you'd have seen a real pro in action just push your butt out a liittttle more and slide down oh you've got it any day now you'll come home late and have to sneak up stairs you'll be a natural oh won't you?"

We had only two steps to go when she turned around and backed down the last two steps like she'd been faking it all along just to keep grandpa happy with this stupid butt-slider method.

Next lesson: Washing dishes and turning out lights. Her mother didn't like either one of them.

§

CHAPTER FIVE

Bits and Pieces

Pig time Daylight Savings

Pulled Over

Retirement Monte Carlo

Singing on Wings of Freedom

Telephones That Crank

The Day After Summer

When I Grow Old

Wood Tick

Hardware Store at Christmas Time

Advertising for Men

A few years ago, I wrote and complained about men not getting equal time on television. It seemed like everything on the screen concerned the weaker sex and a disgusting tendency to develop feminine itch.

If it wasn't two very attractive young women calmly discussing feminine itch, then it was one woman squirming on a chair in a business meeting wishing she'd used Preparation H for her hemorrhoids. Me too. Wishing she had, that is. That way, I wouldn't have had to watch her squirm.

All this is bad enough, but then add in what must be the bottomless billion-dollar market for sanitary products, and it becomes obvious: men aren't much value as consumers. Maybe one of the reasons is that men don't have a hydraulic system that falls apart every 28 days. The truth is, if a tractor hydraulic system did that, we'd fix it. Women, however, have been kind of putting up with what has to be considered kind of a primitive way to lay an egg since time began. Even chickens could be accused of having a better life. I suppose all this is going to fall by the wayside once the new pill comes out that stretches their 28 days out to three months. Pretty quickly, we'll be seeing those ads, one would suppose.

What men need is to go bald every 28 days, because male baldness is the only real market that industry has aimed at, and it isn't big enough to really compete with either feminine napkins (Napkins? Who thought that label up?) or feminine itch.

Maybe if the old male prostate went creaky and wept some noxious emissions that required periodical mopping up, we'd be more on the minds of the advertising geniuses, and could get equal air time. We're not sales worthy, bottom line.

Admittedly, there was a furious burst of advertising activity a while back when Viagra came out, but it didn't last too long, not even when their competition came out with something that they said was better. How could something that increases erectile function be better? That's like saying someone is "more pregnant." Better in this case seems kind of irrelevant. The bottom line is: seven Viagra pills are consumed every second in the USA, according to something I read that pulled sales figures together and divided it by the number of men in this country. All I have to say is that there is some guy somewhere must be using eight.

Maybe what men need to do is concentrate on the things that we do well, like having heart attacks. We could work on having one like once a month. That'd give Madison Avenue a good working goal. "Men! That monthly heart attack got you down? Does it make you feel 'not so masculine?' Want to cure it in three days? Buy our new Kotex anti-seizure pills. Swallow one every morning."

The ad could go on to say: "No other cholesterol-absorbing pill will give you the assurance you need to go out there and play extreme contact basketball or lay concrete blocks with the guys all day, and let you eat greasy fried food and drink beer every night."

Now that's an ad. Men would jump at something like that. "I can't be having a heart attack," the man gasped as the early responders hit him with 40,000 volts, "I've been on the pad."

It's generally agreed that men don't go to the doctor enough. Maybe Madison Avenue could do something about that by advertising an In-Home Cholesterol Test, or an In-Home Baldness Test. These tests would show you, even when you're still in your twenties, whether or not you're going to develop some of these reasons to go see your physician.

In the back of one of the magazines to which I subscribe is an advertisement that is trying to compete with women. It says: "Hernia appliances for comfort! You too can enjoy heavenly comfort night and day and at work or play! 13 million men know. Ask for our free book."

Free book? What the hell do we need a free book for? Women's sanitary napkins don't advertise a free book, and that particular design and insertion problem is considerably more complicated than a bulge somewhere below your belly button. You see, right there is the problem: Men with hernias are stupider than women with menstrual abilities. I'm truly shocked by this insinuation. I watch women parade around on television all night with high-tech bras that look like they'd need an engineering manual. They don't need a book, and they're trying to assemble this gadget around not one but two bulges.

Men have to have a book to cover one little one? What would such a book say? This is the front? This is the back? What about before there was a book. Did men run around with this hernia thing on backwards, wondering why it didn't work? Why they didn't feel so fresh?

So here's the deal: For every feminine ad, I want a masculine one. Every time I see a push-up bra, I want some guy with a big beer belly parading around in his underwear. "I never feel really drunk unless I'm wearing my Hanes."

Would someone care to explain a vacuum treatment for impotence?

§

Dynamite

Two well drilling rigs worked steadily in the sweltering Iowa heat, up on the top of the 60-foot-high quarry cliff face. They drilled rows of 60-foot-deep holes, into which we would pack three-inch-by-two-foot sticks of dynamite on blast day. These explosives would then, when detonated, blast the limestone cliff face loose so that the smaller rock could be picked up by a huge loader, and dumped into a rock crusher.

It was 1962, that summer I worked for this rock crushing outfit. It was a good college summer job. A lot of it was boring, and hot, but then came blasting day. Then it was still hot. But it sure wasn't boring.

Shorty Buckmeyer was the foreman, a short wiry fellow, not an extra ounce of weight on him. He resembled, in more ways than one, a banty rooster, but one that you didn't want to cross.

He acted that way, puffed up, most of the time, except for blasting day, when we had to handle the dynamite.

TNT fumes make people sick. It gives them—us—headaches; it makes them—us-- throw up. It makes you really, really sick, especially in the summer heat, when the stuff oozes liquid nitroglycerin from its skin. The dynamite of course had to be kept locked up in a special, windowless extra-secure building, and when it was 90 degrees outside, which happened in Iowa easily, it was double that in that building, and the fumes were a big problem for us.

Anyway, Shorty spent the first part of blast day daring that dynamite to make him sick, and the second half of it throwing up. Some of us joined him. It's hard for a foreman to maintain leadership qualities when he's bent over behind a gravel truck barfing. Blasting day was hard on Shorty.

Shorty and the owner somehow heard about nitrogen fertilizer and fuel oil, and that it apparently made a pretty explosive mixture. Cheap, too. Buy it all at the local Co-op. When he told us this, we thought he was crazy. He said: "Boys, we're gonna try it."

Next thing you know, it's blasting day, we're up there on that high cliff face, looking at five rows of sixty-foot-deep bore holes, each row a hundred feet long, with twenty-some holes in each row. The drive of the truck seems confused about what he's doing up there. Apparently, he thinks we should know. It's also apparent that we do not. We're all discussing how much granular nitrogen for the Co-op fertilizer truck to auger into each hole. This particular detail? No one had a clue. We philosophized our way to filling the holes one-third full. One hundred-some holes. One-third looked pretty empty, so we poured some more in. What the heck.

We arrived at the amount of fuel oil the same way, hosed in ten gallons into each hole, stood around looking down into them, thought they looked pretty dry, dumped some more in.

Us? With no dynamite to make us sick? We thought we finally had it made. No headaches, no Shorty or any of us throwing up here and there? Pretty easy to take. As we loaded the holes, there was lots of jokes about planting corn in the fertilizer. None of us really thought this was going to work.

Since each time we blasted—about once a week—the electric detonator cord got twenty feet or so shorter, we drew for short straw to see who operated the plunger on the electric detonator. For once, Shorty lost.

One thing. You can't blow all those holes at once, or rock is pushed out across the floor of the quarry. You have to blow the middle and back rows first, so time delay electric caps are installed in the holes. The front row gets the biggest time delay. That way, the front row holds the back rows in place during the blast, and instead of smearing all that rock across the quarry floor—which is a bugger to scrape back up—it kind of piles it up in one big heap. To install the fuses and cap the holes with clay, we took off all metal objects, shoes, jewelry, anything that might generate a static spark. It was a truly hair-raising feeling to walk around up there, knowing how much explosive power lay beneath your feet.

We got it all fused and capped, and, from what we judged was a safe distance away from the blast, about a football field and a half, we watched Shorty raise the dump box of a gravel truck, climb up underneath it for a shield, hook up the det cord to the electric plunger, and holler: "Fire in the hole." We could barely hear him, we were that far away, standing in Johance's alfalfa field.

His arms went up. Then down. As usual, there was a slight delay between the down of his arms and the blast.

Then all Hell broke loose. It became immediately apparent that we had way over estimated the amount of fuel and fertilizer necessary for this. As the mushroom cloud formed, we were for once struck silent with awe. Not one smart remark. All summer we had seen blasts. But never never one this big. The air shock wave hit us like a hammer. We were silent, unbelieving at the ferocity of what we had triggered.

At first the wind blew the cloud away from Shorty, but then it changed and the cloud headed his way. That cloud was pure poison, full of toxic fumes. Shorty took off running, just barely ahead of the cloud. From our position, we found our voices and hollered encouragement. Stuff like: "Run you short-legged little excuse for a rooster!" "Give'er Hell, Shorty!" And so forth. Most of it isn't printable. We were all glad we hadn't gotten the short straw.

It was a grand moment during which no one had quite yet assimilated the size of this blast, nor the fact that we had no doubt just strewn the entire cliff face across the floor of the quarry about six inches thick, a lot of work, hot quarry work.

I heard something whistle, during all this hoo-rawing. Then a whistle again, slightly higher in pitch. Then yet again. Suddenly, with a great loud !!WHOOOMPP!!, a car-sized boulder struck in the hay field about twenty yards away from us.

To heck with Shorty. It was then every man for himself, and we all took off running in every direction, as rocks and boulders of all sizes and descriptions rained down on that farmer's hay field.

When the dust finally cleared, and we surveyed the scene, we found that the blast, which was in a quarry somewhat at the intersection of four gravel roads, had knocked the REA's electric wires down in all four directions, had buried the roads in limestone to the point that it took two bulldozers all one day to clear them, and dropped enough rocks and boulders on Johance's hay field that we picked rock for two days.

Unbelievably, no one got hurt. Well, Shorty's pride took a licking, but we cut the next blast dose by over half, and it worked pretty well.

It was 1962. I was 18 years old. It was very exciting.

§

Burma Shave

SLOW DOWN PA
SAKES ALIVE
MA MISSED SIGNS
FOUR AND FIVE
BURMA SHAVE

From 1925 to 1963, it was difficult if not impossible to find an American anywhere who hadn't seen the Burma-Shave's individual signs in the ditches along the roads of America.

Children in a car could be kept ruly for miles and miles by the mere promise that, just over the hill, was another set of signs, better stop quarrelling and pay attention, you'll miss them. And when they did come, the entire car would shout the verses out loud.

In 1925, Allan Odell, one of two sons of Clinton Odell, who himself founded Burma-Shave, hammered the Burma Shave sign into the dirt alongside the road from

Minneapolis to Red Wing. SHAVE THE MODERN WAY/ FINE FOR THE SKIN/ DRUGGISTS HAVE IT/ BURMA-SHAVE.

From then until the early sixties, the distinctive and friendly signs spread across America until they seemed to be everywhere. Why? Because they sold shaving cream beyond the Odell's wildest dreams. Their light-hearted rhymes were a bright spot in the darkness of the depression. Most importantly, the autos of those times were slow enough to allow the driver and the passengers to read the signs. Anywhere there was a straight stretch of road, Burma-Shave's humor could have your attention for a few seconds, an advertising miracle.

The signs evolved through the years, moving with the country's progress. HE PLAYED A SAX/ HAD NO B.O./ HIS WHISKERS SCRATCHED/ SHE LET HIM GO/ BURMA-SHAVE.

FROM NEW YORK CITY/ TO PUMPKIN HOLLER/ ITS HALF A POUND/ FOR HALF A DOLLAR/ BURMA-SHAVE.

The war came along, and along came such verses as: TESTED IN PEACE/ PROVEN IN WAR/ BETTER NOW/ THAN BEFORE/ BURMA-SHAVE. AT EASE SHE SAID/ MANEUVERS BEGIN/ WHEN YOU GET THOSE WHIS-KERS/ OFF YOUR CHIN/ BURMA-SHAVE.

As the speed of cars increased, the little signs had to be made larger, and spaced farther apart, so the readers had time to catch them all. Public safety messages began to show up in the little signs, because accidents began to increase. Remember when we actually thought car accidents could be totally erased? We had won the war, harnessed the atom, broken the sound barrier. Everyone saw their children's lives much improved over their own. Nothing, absolutely nothing, was impossible. All we had to do was give it our best.

PAST SCHOOLHOUSES/ TAKE IT SLOW/ LET THE LITTLE/ SHAV-ERS GROW/ BURMA-SHAVE. The little signs raised punning, alliteration, and double-meaning to a science, all in the name of safety. And of course raised selling Burma-Shave to a new high.

When I was growing up, I remember the signs. There were some on High-way 9, in Iowa, close to us. I also remember the "X marks the spot" safety campaign to alert passing motorists to danger spots on the highway. Large white crosses were placed where ever someone had been killed. Burma-Shave got in the act: SPEED/ WAS HIGH/ WEATHER WAS NOT/ TIRES WERE THIN/ X MARKS THE SPOT/ BURMA-SHAVE. DON'T LOSE YOUR HEAD/ TO GAIN A MINUTE/ YOUR NEED YOUR HEAD/ YOUR BRAINS ARE IN IT/ BURMA-SHAVE.

Soon, there were so many gory clusters of white X's that the program was abandoned. Deaths didn't diminish. The crosses did.

The signs became more stringent: IT'S BEST FOR ONE/ WHO HITS THE BOT-TLE/ TO LET ANOTHER/ USE THE THROTTLE/ BURMA-SHAVE.

And so they didn't leave women out of it: HER CHARIOT RACE/ AT 80 PER/ THEY HAULED AWAY/ WHAT HAD BEN HUR/ BURMA-SHAVE.

Car accidents didn't stop. The only thing that really slowed down in the late fifties and early sixties was the sale of Burma-Shave. They never were able to target the large urban areas where so many people began to cluster. The signs were themselves a sign of a rural era, an era that faded away as people moved to cities. Finally, Phillip Morris Co. bought Burma-Shave in 1963.

The Smithsonian Museum has one of the last set of signs to exist in this country, although die-hard motorists still swear there are some left out there, way out in the boondocks.

Burma-Shave kept their tongue in their cheek right up to the end. This set of signs was donated to the Smithsonian: SHAVING BRUSHES/ YOU'LL SOON SEE'UM/ ON THE SHELF/ IN SOME MUSEUM/ BURMA-SHAVE.

Maybe we lost more than Burma-Shave signs.

Maybe we lost some of our sense of humor back there, too.

§

Class Reunion

So what is it we expect to see at our umpteenth class reunion? Hair with more grey in it than our own? Hair with more hair in it than our own?

Do we go to see who aged the most, or to see who didn't? Who got prettier? Who didn't?

Or maybe we don't go at all, because no matter how hard we try, we cannot see a reason to add one more mountain to our summer climbing schedule. Over half of my class didn't show up to one I just went to. Maybe there isn't just one reason for people not to go; maybe there are several, and they gang up, until they become too powerful, and you just stay home and watch TV.

What do you talk about to someone you haven't seen in umpteen years? "Hi," you might start out with, "how do you feel about being fatter-balder-greyer-older than the rest of us?" That would be a good conversation starter. Be sure and smile. If you're going to point out warts, a smile might not be quite enough; better throw in a pat on the back, too.

Another conversation starter might be: "Boy, the President really sucks, doesn't he?" Based on current political bipartisanship statistics, that one has at least a one in two chance of not getting you into a humdinger of a debate, but plan on moving from group to group frequently. Work on your short snorts of derision, and prepare to nod knowingly, no matter what someone says, and use this one: "Well, you know what Abraham Lincoln—Albert Einstein—Mother Teresa said about that," then move on, before they find out you don't know what anybody said about anything.

Maybe there are other reasons to go to your class reunion. Maybe your wife wants to have one more go at that blond tart you went with back in high school. You know the one. She wrote you those love letters that you thought were long gone, the long fuzzy rambling ones about how fine you were? The ones that your wife found the ninth year of your marriage. Remember that tenth reunion?

Remember the year leading up to it? The year your wife started using the cutesey-wutesey pet names for you that were in the letters? "Shouldn't we get ready for church, love bunny?" Or she would look at you over the kitchen table and say, "My, your body is fine like wine, sweet cheeks." That was a long year. A long, long, long year.

Life sure sends some stumbling blocks, doesn't it. You and your wife at the reunion found your place card right across the table from your old flame, and she was looking fine. Had on that red dress she was busting out of and those high heels that said: "Ask me to dance; I'm all yours again."

Your wife had on a dress that said: "I've had three kids, and gravity is winning. You know it. I know it. I hate you. Let's fight."

All you remember was the first thing she said to that hussy, which was something like: "They don't take out the trash here at all, do they?" Whooeee. Now, that was a reunion from hell.

But wait! Maybe–just maybe-- you go to your reunion to see the high school sweetheart that you haven't seen in over half a lifetime, the one from whom you were separated for reasons you cannot exactly recall anymore. Maybe it wasn't avoidable. Maybe it should have been. Maybe, maybe, maybe. Life has a lot of maybes.

She might be there, you know. Maybe.

She might well be there. She might show up. Maybe.

She might be alone, standing somewhere across the room, and you might walk over to her, wondering all the hundred lifetimes it takes you to get over there exactly what in the world you're going to say to her. You close the distance with a few final steps, and then you're standing in front of her.

Maybe that's when she smiles, and you remember why you were attracted to her in the first place. Then you remember what it's like to stand in the shine of a hundred watt smile framed by silver dollar dimples. Memories drill holes right through you. Your mouth opens, and your thoughts leak out and evaporate into nothingness, and you smile, and mutter something, and feel seventeen again.

Maybe then you remember how easy she is to talk to, when you start talking again, and as you talk, it's almost like you've never been away, and maybe then you're suddenly glad you came.

High school class reunions.

Maybe.

§

Cleaning the Tractor Toolbox

It's that time of the year when the promise of spring overrides an underlying but upsetting message that nothing is permanent. Winter isn't permanent. Summer isn't either. Not much is. Oh, maybe politics is permanent. That doesn't seem to change. And the arrogance of the French. They can be counted on, mostly. But the fact doesn't go away that summer means winter is coming, and then winter means summer is coming.

Sometimes, at this time of the year, you need something. For me, that's an old tractor, one that is at least fifty years old; one I can look at and say, at least to myself: "That damned thing made it. I'm here leaning on it; I must be making it, too."

There's something about the assurance of an old tractor's large solid unchanging bulk that led me out to the tractor shed the other day, led me out there a few weeks ago on a crisp morning behind the balloon that my breath formed. I plugged in the portable oil heater, and just leaned against the tractor. I missed that tractor all winter, but I didn't miss it, if you know what I mean.

I noticed the yawning lid of the toolbox behind the steering wheel, which came mounted on the used tractor when I bought it thirty years ago. It occurred to me that I had never been able to close it for the junk it held. I decided to clean that tool box.

It didn't take me long to feel what I think an archaeologist must feel as they dig down through successive layers of civilization's remains.

Only instead of pots and pans and arrowheads, I found, in the order that the artifacts surfaced, two empty oil cans, the old kind that you squirt oil with. One was missing its snout, and the other the squeeze handle, they weren't much good.

Then I found three old socks that had been used for grease rags. I had wondered where they'd went. So it wasn't my washing machine that had been eating them after all. It was the tractor. One wonders how.

I found countless rusty, barely recognizable and completely unusable square nuts, bolts, washers, pins, keys, chain links and such, each embedded in the hard packed bed of field soil which suspended all this stuff in a kind of prehistoric sea bed.

I found a single gopher trap, severely mauled. I vaguely remembered the neighbor boy coming over to trap gophers in my hay field several years ago. He set six traps. Found five. I found the sixth one just when the sky was threatening rain and I still had half the field to cut. It took two hours to repair the damage to the mower.

There was one half-inch box end wrench. In fact, it was the only functional tool in the tool box, looking out of place amongst the broken screwdrivers, cracked sockets, and three pliers rusted into petrified uselessness. Then I saw the imported adjustable wrench that I had picked up off the blacktop road a long time ago. I remembered stopping and gleefully picking it up, and then the first time I used it, having it slip on a nut and take a big hunk of skin off a finger. Due to some Law of Something, for years it was the only tool I could ever find when I needed one. For a long time it wouldn't go away. It was a malicious metal monster that insisted on hanging around and being the only tool I could find and chewing the skin off my knuckles. There it was. Apparently the tool box had caught it sleeping, and had absorbed it.

I found the mashed cardboard tube from an empty roll of toilet paper. Signs of civilization.

I found a really mean looking spike, one that I was sure some past farmer had dug out of a flat rear tire, just as the last of the weight-adding fluid ran out onto the ground, which is about when the co-op's tire truck usually arrived. I'm sure that the disgruntled farmer, knowing that the toolbox never gave up its dead, threw it in there.

Finally, clear down at the bottom of the box, I found several old wooden "farmer" matches. I really thought about them, and what they were for. Finally, it came to me: Some past farmer had struck those matches to illuminate the early search for what still is the never ending quest for the perfect farm program.

Or maybe he smoked.

I was done. I looked at the now empty tool box. It didn't look right. I threw all the junk back into the box, and went back into the house. The lid wouldn't close.

Some things shouldn't change.

§

Gopher Burn

Well, it's spring, and it's gopher trapping time again, out here in the country, where the little buggers, full of energy after sleeping all winter, are building dirt mounds steep enough to tip over a tank.

One breeding pair of gophers can produce up to 88 more in one summer. They're a simple little animal. They can't see. They can't run. Don't fly. Don't vote. Can't tie their own shoelaces. Probably have an IQ comparable to a stick.

Then why can't I catch them? It should be an embarrassingly lopsided contest, me with a couple of college degrees against a blind rodent. But it isn't. Oh sure. They stick their sick and lame in my traps on a rare occasion so that I don't escalate and use the nuclear option, but that's about it. According to my math, they're gaining on me 80 at a time.

This war with gophers goes back to the first 10 apple trees that I planted. Word spread underground, fresh apple roots, and they came by the busloads. Some of them came up from China through a tunnel exchange program, just so they could get in on the fun. The day after the trees were planted, they'd poke their heads up every few minutes, spit out a fresh mouthful of tunnel dirt onto my lawn, and go back down for more. Every day when I got up, one more apple tree was tipped over, its roots gnawed off.

One day, when no one else here was home, I declared war. Usually, if anyone else is around, I don't let the real me out, the gopher-hating, tunnel-invading, rodent-war-mongering madman. No one was home. For this first action, I needed guns, lots of guns. Shotguns. Rifles. Pistols. I had twenty rounds for the .22; 11 rounds for the .410; and three shells for the 12-gauge pump shotgun. I grabbed them all.

Hitting them with the .22 was impossible. A little bullet like that, even a faint breath of wind probably blows it off course. Maybe the barrel was crooked. Those rounds were gone pretty quickly. It was like a carnival, little heads popping up here and there, popping back down, over here, over there, behind me.

I loaded the .410. It also seemed to have a crooked barrel.

I tried different tactics. Pretended to be picking apples, but instead whirled and fired at retracting heads. There were so many of them. All the whirling about made me dizzy.

Then I pretended to be going back to the house—the old "I'm giving up" strategy, and then firing over my shoulder. I got the rear tire on the riding mower. Finally, I was down to the three shells for the 12-gauge. I laid down on the ground, lined up three little pop-up heads in a row, and fired. Fired again. Gave'em another one.

An examination of the battlefield revealed no gopher corpses. They must take away their dead. My side had two casualties: the riding mower tire, and one apple tree, sliced off by the shotgun.

I put away those deadly tools of destruction, and went and got a can of gasoline and a can of diesel fuel. Oh, and a lighter. Here's how this works. First, you dig open the end hole in a line of holes. Then you dig open the far hole. Into one hole, you pour a slug of gasoline. Into the other, you pour diesel fuel. Once the diesel fuel is lit, the draft pulls gasoline fumes into the tunnel, through the enemy's living room, along with enough air to provide a combustible amount of oxygen. When the two meet, there's a most satisfying "WHUUUMMMPPPP!!!!"

I lit off three of these, and went in to lunch. Before I even had the grilled cheese sandwich done on both sides, their troops were digging again, in the very holes which I had just burned.

I raced outside with more gasoline and diesel fuel and opened up at least two dozen tunnels, and this time poured in enough gasoline and diesel fuel to set the entire township on fire. I raced around with the lighter, but in the smoke and flames, I became confused and as I was crossing one tunnel opening, it exploded and set my pants on fire. I spilled the last of the gasoline as I was beating on my legs. It caught fire. That scorched my hair and took off the eyebrow on one side of my face. Two more secondary tunnel explosions went off.

About then, the mailman came up the driveway, which he does when he has a large package. He turned the bend at the top of the driveway and looked around. He saw guns laying all over the lawn, and me dancing around trying to put out my pants. I saw him and tried to suddenly act normal. Around me, it looked like someone had invaded the Iraqi oil fields and set them on fire. There were dozens of oil well smoke plumes rising thickly in the air.

"Hi there," I said to him. Another explosion went off behind me. He flinched.

"Package," he said. He threw it out the window and reversed all the way back down the driveway.

Everything is cleaned up again. Except for the fresh mounds of dirt that come every day, things look normal.

When no one is looking, I practice whirling and shooting.

§

Guy Stuff

In a confused daze, I decided to call the Head Psychoanalyst of The Tribe of Guys. I didn't know where else to turn. I thought by now I'd have a lot more answers than I do. I thought by now that even slow learners would have figured out the basics about this particular subject.

I wanted The Head Psychoanalyst to explain women to me. I've tried on my own. I've decided aliens would be easier to understand. At least they wouldn't use the same alphabet, and lead you to thinking you heard what they said.

I dialed. His secretary answered. It was a woman. When one calls up the Head Psycho of The Tribe of Guys, one expects a man. Now a woman.

"Whaddya want?" she asked, and the sound of her voice reminded me of a ball bearing I once had go out on the front wheel of my car.

"Well," I replied, "I called to ask The Head Psycho a question." I didn't tell her the question. A sudden thought came to me. "Say," I asked her, "you're not The Head Psycho, are you?" That'd be a kick in the butt, have The Head Psycho of The Tribe of Guys be a woman.

"No," she said, "but I screen all his calls." She was smiling. You know? You can tell when someone you cannot see is smiling. They've got this kind of sneer to their voice.

"I need to talk to him," I said. I tried to keep desperation out of my voice. Women sense fear, and move right in.

"What's the subject matter; you have to tell me that at least," she said. Suddenly, I remembered the time I went to the doctor with what I thought was a prostate infection. It turned out it was a prostate infection. The doctor found that out. The doctor was a she. When I'm The President of The Tribe of Guys, there'll be some laws about what and what and when and where a she doctor can probe.

It was bad enough when I walked into the clinic, and the receptionist asked me what was wrong. I told her I wasn't sure. I really was sure, but I was stalling. Then she asked me where it hurt. I told her it hurt at home, in the car on the way here, and now it hurts in the waiting room. I finally convinced her I was an idiot, and she let me sit down.

I think there was A Guy Doctor in the house, and she gave me to The Girl Doctor just to be mean. There are a lot of bad things to be said about the male prostate; another one would be having aliens inspecting it.

Now I'm on the phone, I need to talk to The HP, and it's kind of the same thing. If I tell this female what I want to know, well—there's such a thing as too much truth. I've lived my life by this "Too Much Truth" creed. I'll give you an example.

Once, the drummer's girlfriend kissed me. I'm the piano player. Everyone wants to kiss the piano player. Or shoot him. One of the two. This time I got kissed.

Now, the problem is: If I go home and tell The Old Girl I've been kissed, then by the very telling it means it must be important, for after all, you wouldn't tell something to someone if it wasn't important. Now you've gone and made something that wasn't important, important. Just bear with me.

On the other hand, if you don't tell her—because it's not important, right?--, then it's become important because obviously to the opposite sex it appears that you thought it might be if you told it, so you didn't. You see the dilemma here? So I usually opted for the path of least output. In other words, I didn't say anything.

The next day, she found out somehow, and it became Real Important. Even though I used my creed logic on her, and took Guy Logic to new heights, she still got pretty chilly.

I've tried this logic out on other people, and it seems to work. It works real good on other guys. Other guys actually appreciate it. Matter of fact, other guys often say: "Just cut to the bottom line here, so I can go fishing, or snow mobile riding, or drinking, or whatever." They don't see the need to make stuff complicated.

If there's something they don't think you need to know, great.

So, I told The Ball Bearing this: "My car pulls to the right; maybe The HP knows what's wrong with it."

I won't know any more about women, but it'd be nice to at least have a car that drives straight.

§

Letter Alongside the Road

I find a lot of interesting stuff alongside the road where I walk on the evenings when I don't go swimming. Old shoes lie there solo, their other foot now in some other part of the world. Their pose—in the road, often right side up—seems to refute the knowledge that they are unwanted now, that they are of value only as a couple. Old shoes, like people, seem to ache with empty feelings.

There are lots of empty beer cans and liquor bottles, a continuous reminder that a civilized society picks and chooses its drugs like it picks and chooses its wars, ignoring their grinding effect on human decency and mortality, relying more on the traditional basis that history in the form of our ancestors drank and warred, and if it was good for them, it must be good for us, too.

Sometimes there's an explosion of plastic and glass and other parts of the front end of a car, where some luckless deer stepped into some luckless car's path and proved to someone once again that the good day you were having just a moment ago—which you didn't really think was in fact all that good—really in fact was good, compared to the one now with the five-hundred-dollar deductible you were going to have to cough up. One tenth of a second either way, and your bad day was a good day, for both you and the deer.

The other day, I found the torn-up remains of a hand-written letter. It was bunched up enough that I could put some of the fragments together into larger fragments, and almost read the intent behind them. Not quite. But almost.

"Dear Jo…," began the letter. Ah, a Dear John letter, and this time the john's name really is John. I assembled a couple more pieces.

"You know that I'll…" Let's see: "You know that I'll…miss you?" "…pay your bail as soon as I get back from the casino with it?" "…hate you for the rest of my life, which I hope is a lot longer than yours?" "…regret not handcuffing you to the bed and…." "…always regret not leaving you before the sixth child was born?" "…miss you each time the preacher and I are ordering rum on the beaches of the Monte Carlo?" "…send you the money I stole from the kids as soon as I hit the Lotto?" "…try and not hate you while you're dying of the Upper Japanese River Fever?" "…always regret not telling you I had AIDS?"

Well, ok then. I read on, frantically assembling pieces for more information. This was turning out to be like a book from which someone had stolen the last ten pages; like a bad soap opera, or an addiction to "Lost," the TV show. I quit walking, turned my back to the wind and the cars speeding by, and frantically tried to assemble some more of it.

"When I first met you, …" When I first met you? "When I first met you, … you were a stud with your cigarettes rolled up in your tee-shirt sleeve." "…you had just knocked up my sister." "…your teeth needed some work, especially the ones that were missing." "…I thought I'd never rob a bank." "…your breath stank like a Hindu's gym shoe." "…you were just getting out of jail for…" "…I should have shot you then, because I'd be out of jail by now." "…you said your band needed a singer and I should try out, but you never said it was to be the groupie."

I needed more information. I tried different torn pieces in different combinations. Another somewhat legible sentence popped out: "I guess I should…" "I guess I should…have known you went to family reunions for dates." "…have guessed you weren't a preacher." "…have told you I was only fifteen." "…have warned you that daddy would use a shotgun to force you to marry me." "…have told you I had a bad gambling habit before I sold our house." "…have told you that when I'm driving, I usually hit six deer each year." "…that I had just had my gastric bypass undone, because I'd rather weigh four hundred pounds and be happy."

The last part that I managed to put together started with: "I'll always…" "I'll always…wonder what life would have been like if you hadn't taken after me with a chain saw and cut off both my legs but I still love you and miss you." "…take good care of your Harley Davidson because my cousin and I are really truly in love and we're leaving on it." "…be sorry that you're in jail for that little something that I left in the car and the cops found."

Sigh. There's nothing like a nice love letter.

§

Librarian Bar Codes

"GET YOURSELF BARCODED HERE!" said the sign hanging in the window of the local library.

It used to be such a nice, quiet little library, nestled semi-comatosely within the smothering oneness of a nice, quiet little town, where all the women have dainty feet, and all the students are on the honor rolls.

It used to be. It isn't any more. What I predicted would happen has come true: Modern data tracking devices have come and ruined everything. They're gone and not only taken away my name—can't sign your name anymore, young man, just your number—but then to make it worse, they've snatched my number now, too.

It took them forty years to get my name away from me. Then they gave me a number. That only lasted about two years. "Just sign your number right here," the library used to say. "We don't want anyone to know private stuff."

Heck, that's how I knew whether a book was any good, by who had read it.

Now I have to get bar coded. Why? By the time I get up tomorrow morning, what'll be next? It's worrisome.

At the time, when they wanted to turn me into a number and quit signing my name on the check-out card, they said: "It's a policy thing."

What policy thing, I asked? Why is it bad policy to want to use the name my mama gave to me, the one that I've gotten used to all these years. And it's used to me. That's a policy thing too, isn't it? My policy.

"Well, sir," she said to me….

No. Please, I said. I've just had another policy change. "Sir" was my father's name. Don't call me that. I've decided you should indeed call my by a number, and I choose "Seven." I told her that I've always had a soft spot for seven. Seven dwarves. Seven seas that someday I'm going to sail. Seven pheasants used to be the bag limit before we decimated the population. And of course at the age of seven I had my first…

She got up from her chair there behind the big counter, and huffed off to the head librarian's office. This younger woman came out. She walked toward me a bit stiffly, probably from lugging all those books around when she went to librarian school.

"Is there a problem?" she asked. Her tone of voice said that she knew there was a problem, ok, and she was looking at it.

Well, yes, there might be a problem, I said. I might be related to Dewey, who invented the Dewey Decimal system. If it was a good policy enough for him, I began to say.…

She interrupted. Asked what my name was again?

I told her my name was 1.223.0401. I just said I might be related to a Dewey. What did she expect?

She started to say something, but I interrupted her.

Please, I said. All my friends call me one point two.

She said, "Sir," (Evidently my name policy about "sir" is going to be harder to comprehend that I first estimated.) "We here at The Library are faced with the task of hauling Neanderthals such as yourself kicking and convulsing into the twenty first century. That's why we're bar coding you now." There. Now she had told him. Gave him the truth. Her head ache threatened to worsen.

I said to her: You can't give me a barcode. Back when you gave me a number, I had all sorts of problems. The bank wouldn't cash checks that I signed one point two whatever. People didn't know me. It took ma six phone calls before she figured out that her son was the one point two that was calling collect.

Poor thing. Now look what you're going to put her through. She'll answer the phone and ask: "Who is this?"

I'll say it's (EDITOR: PLEASE PASTE A BAR CODE HERE.).

She'll say, "Who? Did you say (EDITOR: PLEASE PASTE A DIFFERENT BAR CODE HERE.)?

I'll say, no, not him. You always did say we sounded alike. I'm (THE FIRST BAR CODE HERE, PLEASE.)

"Who?" Her voice will be near panic. She's not young like she used to be when we called each other names.

I'll say: Well, you know who. Then I'll whisper: "one point two." But now, I'll tell her, you have to call me (BAR CODE HERE.)

The head librarian stamped one of her dainty undersized feet, and turned away to walk off. Before she left, though, she said BAR CODE THIS: !!$@%#^$&%*^!!! Oh my.

§

Mustard Plaster

As long, cold winters like this one go slowly on and grudgingly build the extra minutes of sunshine every day that will eventually rescue us from brainlessly deciding to stay and live at this awful latitude, we all search for solace.

Solace from what? There is one group of organisms that loves this latitude, loves bunches of people sealed up in air-tight boxes where there is always one human that believes he and he alone will enter the Guinness World Book of Records with this sneeze. You've seen these humans. Their faces begin The Sneeze Wrinkle. That wrinkle gives them time to develop a lung full of air. They cock their head back, look up at a bright light to more sharply trigger this expulsion of snot and air, and fire it into the room.

Right where you are.

The fact that murder rates drop up here in the winter doesn't make sense.

Something else doesn't make sense: I haven't had one single common cold this winter, not one. Not one sinus infection, flu germ, or stomach flu. As this winter passes the two-thirds mark, and I have a chance for a personal best at this germ-free record, perhaps murder will become an alternative, when I maul some hapless sneezer.

As it is, all conversations with friends begins with: "Hey. Come on up (from the Twin Cities, breeding place for contagious enemies) and we'll go sliding." After a second more, I add: "You're not sick, are you?"

Unspoken are the words: "Cause if you are, you're sleeping in the garage."

Of course they know I'm joking. They should also know that I'll love them just as much in the garage as in the house.

Back when I was a kid, germs were treated much more seriously, because antibiotics and doctor visits were pretty rare, and no one knew for sure which germ might progress to something so serious that a doctor might be involved. Grown-ups from that era, the late forties and early fifties, remembered quite well the fact that doctors used to be barbers who learned their trade while practicing taking out tonsils and teeth. They remembered doctors before doctors even had official medical colleges where they learned stuff that could really kill you.

There are two medical treatments that parents knew which I remember. One happened when you as a child became so hoarse with a sore throat that you couldn't even bluff a normal speaking voice anymore. Your life began to take a major turn for the worse when you came into the kitchen and saw dad with a goose feather in one hand and the iodine bottle in the other.

He didn't even say anything, just beckoned you with one finger. And just like that, you knew there was no place to run, no place to hide. There was nothing left to do but slowly, veeeery slowly walk over there.

"Say 'ahhhhh'," he would tell you. Then with a dip of the tip of the feather in the iodine so quick that it must be magic, he stuck it down your gullet and coated all the red goopy soreness down there in one swipe.

I asked him later, once I was grown up and he couldn't catch me anymore, could he coat everything in one swipe, and he said: "I had to do it in one, one was the only chance you got."

That's for sure. I remember long minutes of gagging, which I'm sure I accentuated for extra pity. There was no pity. They'd grown up with the medical feather; they were happy to get the chance to use it on someone else. "Let's have kids," I can hear my parents telling each other, "so we can gag them with The Feather."

Seriously, they also knew that, without antibiotics, kids got sick and died, even though the same parents ended up with a bill for removal of tonsils. Better the feather.

Or the mustard plaster. Now, there's a method for making errant foreign terrorists cough up the truth. Let's restrain'em, and slap one of these on their chest. They'd talk.

The only good thing about the mustard plaster was that at least, mom did it. With dad, you kind of felt that you could as easily be a calf or baby pig. He apparently didn't care which, just went ahead with a certain calm, stoic attitude.

Mom knew, and you could tell. "This will feel hot, but it'll make you feel better."

Hot? Hot is fire. This was way past fire. Which was why she sat beside you at your bedside, and sympathized with you while she held you down, saying things like: "Just think how much better you'll feel when you're able to breath and run around again."

Uh huh. The thick, mustard-plastered cotton cloth must have been warmed up to a thousand degrees. You could feel it burning your chest skin, you could smell the skin puckering and turning black, and when you thought it couldn't get any worse, then the mustard began to prickle and itch and burn. Ohhhhhhhnooooooooooi'mdyingma!!!!!

Then you woke up the next day ready to run around again. Coughed up about a bucket full of snot the first hour, marveling at the colors of your expectorations while they froze in a snow bank. Instant recovery time.

I hope I don't catch anything. Remedies like that would kill me now.

Call before you come, so I can hear if you're dripping, or coughing, or plugged up.

§

Old Shoes

Someone said to me the other day: "How come you only see one shoe lying on the side of the road?"

Huh. I hadn't thought much about that, until it was brought up. Really. Now, I can't get it out of my mind. Things like that bother me. Stuff like overdrafts from the bank and unpaid bills for new tires just have to wait their turn, faced with choices such as this to worry about.

If I could just get this important stuff figured out, life would be oh so much grander.

About the one shoe, there has to be some good reason it's there. Maybe those of you out there who are missing one could e-mail me and let me know how one got away, and one got to stay. That's assuming you know.

If you don't know how one got away, and one got left behind, it could indicate shoe aliens, or foul play of some sort, like shoe terrorism. After all, airports are highly suspicious of shoes these days. Shoes therefore must be up to something.

When I renewed my home owner's insurance the other day, the nice lady who peers over the huge pile all this paperwork makes on her desk asked me if I wanted to keep the "terrorism rider," or exclude it.

"What kind of terrorism does this cover?" I asked her. There are, after all, all kinds of terrorism. There's psychological terror, like if the septic system inspector comes out and says you're out of compliance and it's going to cost you five grand to get back on the right side of the smell.

There's even the terror of your homeowner's insurance going up twelve percent, which it had.

It turned out that apparently she's gotten a lot of crap over this terrorism exclusion, because she got a bit brittle with me and I signed off on it.

Now I'm a victim of insurance agent terror. Next thing you know, I'll need medication. I hope I'm covered by my policy. I don't dare call her, though. She sounded like maybe she was a terror victim of some sort herself.

What I didn't ask her was if she was aware of any shoe terrorism in the neighborhood. After she snapped, I didn't dare, but I wanted to.

Maybe shoes don't get along 'til death do they part. Maybe they're a lot like the people who wear them, and stuff happens. Maybe they change. Maybe they don't. Maybe shoes have disagreements. Maybe one shoe is male, and the other is female. Maybe there's a lot we don't know about shoes. I could see one shoe saying to the other:

"You philanderer, your tongue was hanging out at that red pump!" This said while laced to the feet of a guy who is at the moment viewing a flat tire on his car.

"I was not. You're the one who's been stepping out, never letting me lead off. I am the right foot, right?" This is an old argument, it's easy to see. You've either got the right stuff, or the left stuff.

"You're the one who walked out, not me. Once a heel, always a heel."
What if the two shoes discover one day that they have completely different philosophies of life, and she says to him: "You don't have a sole."

He says back to her, in a sing-song voice: "There was an old lady who lived in a shoe." That might have quieted her. Not "shoes," just "shoe." Next thing you know, the guy who had the flat tire is changing shoes, and she sees an opportunity, and kicks him out.

It gets even more complicated. Now there's a whole bunch of single shoes abandoned by the side of the road. What are the chances that any of these lost soles are going to find a mate? Who's going to want them? After all, they've worn out their welcome where they were, and now they're old and pretty tattered, beat up, unable to make any new starts. Even if they find another old shoe, they'll worry about matching up.

What if, after lying at the side of the road watching life go by for years and years, they're found and matched back up with their mate? Will they still be a pair, like they used to be? Will they be able to reside peacefully beside one another in their old age, taking it easy in the closet, content to talk about the kicking and pinching and scuffing they've seen while they were apart?

Or will they just be two shoes?

New shoes are attractive, but often pinch.

Old shoes are comfortable, but less fancy.

What if we're all old shoes, someday?

§

Pig Time Daylight Savings

This whole daylight savings time thing has me upset. One wouldn't think that an hourmore or less, here or there, now or then, spring or fall, could have that much impact, but it does.

I've reached an age that, to be honest, there were times I thought I wouldn't reach. The young never consider becoming old. It seems impossible, and therefore not important. More important things take up the minds of the young: The opposite sex, mirrors, the opposite sex, cars and trucks, the opposite sex, and so forth.

Time? Uh uh. Not for the young. Not until you get here, then, at some age, time becomes pretty darned important, which is why I resent people tinkering with it and confusing me. Speaking of time, now would be a good time for my "time" joke.

I was driving along a rural road one day when I looked over and saw a farmer holding a good-sized pig up in the air so the pig could grab an apple off the tree. Then he held the pig while it was chewed up, hoisting him up once again for another apple. I stopped because, well, because time worries me. I climbed the fence and walked over. "Say," I asked, "what are you doing?"

The farmer gave me a look and said: "What does it look like I'm doing? I'm feeding my pigs." There were several more milling around his ankles.

"But," I stated somewhat emphatically, "doesn't this take a lot of time?"

"But," said the farmer back, "what's time to a pig?"

Indeed. Back to the subject: Time becomes more important as one begins to see that it's not going to last forever. I'm beginning to see that. At a young age, exposed to farm tractors, guns and loud rock and roll, I worried that at this age I'd be too deaf to hear St. Peter's call; now, as confused as I am about what time it really is, maybe my time will be up and I won't know.

Which is why I'm worked up over "saving" time, which would seem to be the meaning of "daylight savings time." For one thing, I now find myself eating supper in the middle of the afternoon, which is fine and dandy, except then it seems like I need another meal before I go to bed, which by the clock is about another half day later. My stomach is confused.

My head is confused when I now get up and the sun isn't where it's supposed to be, supper isn't where it's supposed to be, and bedtime isn't, either. Each time I feel like they're where they're supposed to be, I look at a clock and someone has instructed me that they aren't.

What really worries me is that if they can do it once, they can do it again. And who does this, exactly? Is there a Commission on Confusing Time somewhere? Is it the government? If it is the government, don't they have better things to do? Like health care, education, and the budget? Maybe it's true that government has gotten too large if there is a Committee somewhere arguing about whether or not they should "adjust" my clock some more.

I'm concerned that I have no power over any of this. I'm concerned that I'll get up tomorrow and find that my supper, because of some Commission-issued edict, is where lunch used to be. What if there are more Republicans than Democrats on that Committee? Republicans want to cut stuff out, reduce stuff like spending and government in general? A Committee Republican might say: "I make a motion to reduce the 24-hour day to 23 hours, thus saving stuff like printing on plane and train schedules, and when Dexter and Weeds come on the TV." All in favor, etc., etc.

Which hour will they cut out? I'm worried that they'll cut out lunch altogether, which would allow supper to crash into breakfast. Oh, you say, they won't do that.

They won't? If you're so smart, then tell me who's in charge of Staylight Savings Time? Yeah, that's what I mean. That Commission is so buried in Big Government that no one knows where they are, if they did want to complain. It's certainly not hard to understand their desire to remain hidden. I don't know anyone who isn't confused about this time stuff. Their phone would ring off the hook. We'd all be calling to find out what time it really is.

The last thing about all this that really has me upset is I can't figure out if I'm an hour older? Or an hour younger. You know, of course, that the astronauts, because they circle the earth repeatedly at speeds around 18,000 mph, and because Einstein proved that time slows as one speeds up, are approximately one one-hundredth of a second younger when we bring them back to earth.

So don't tell me you cannot lose an hour here or there. Time goes fast.

It'll slip right away on you.

§

Pulled Over

I turned left on a city block and looked in the rear view mirror. There I saw a town cop with his bubble gum flashers all lit up.

I pulled over to the side and stopped to let him by. I had seen him back there at the school intersection, so I, for once, had come to a full stop at the stop sign. So it couldn't be innocent me that he was after. Must be someone ahead of me. He didn't go by. Much less than not go by, he was stopped and getting out of his car and walking up to my car, one hand on his gun.

The little red Geo is little. Looking up at him gave me a crick in my neck. I kept shifting around, trying to ease the pain. OK, so I looked shifty.

By this point in life, I've earned several tickets. Most of us probably have, as far as that goes. Rural stop signs honestly appear to me to be a total waste of time, and an equally great waste of Newton's First Law of Motion, which states that a body in motion wants to remain in motion.

Newton must have never had many stop signs. No one in this century, so full that it is of towns and cities and stop lights and yield signs and automotive congestion, would have ever considered any law except for one that said: A car in motion is unnatural, therefore the Law is: A body at rest wants to remain at rest. Which is the flip side of Newton's First Law, really.

When I'm in motion, and I can see miles in every rural direction, exactly why is it that I must stop? Stopping is more costly to society.

It's more costly because I know we're running short of gasoline. Despite Bush's best efforts to help us in that regard, our gas is still buried under their sand. In a way, me running a stop sign and not wasting gasoline defeating Newton's First Law of Motion is supporting our troops in Iraq. If all of us ran stop signs every chance we could, our national gas mileage would improve.

The cop looked down at me, me sitting down there twitching and rubbing my neck, and asked: "Do you know why I stopped you?"

Do I know why you stopped me? I thought about that to myself.

Then I thought to myself: Although he's pretty young, maybe the same memory thing that seems to afflict me is setting in on him. I get to the bathroom with no apparent reason in mind. I paw through the kitchen junk drawer for several minutes before I realize I don't know why.

Maybe this guy pulled me over, and by the time he walked up to me, realized that he cannot any longer remember why. I wanted to help him, but I was completely unable to. I was the pullee. He was the pullor. He was going to have to figure this out himself.

"You pulled me over because you're going senile like me?"

I didn't say that.

Then I thought to myself, maybe he thinks he's being clever. I peered up at him and continued to wiggle my head to release some of the crick in my neck.

"You pulled me over because I've got a trunk full of cocaine and there's a trail of white powder down the road behind me that ran out through a rust hole in the floor?"

I didn't say that.

"Maybe you pulled me over because you're going to give me a medal of commendation for helping the war effort by running stop signs every time I see one?"

I didn't say that, either. I guess I'm not much of a criminal, because I couldn't come up with anything good to confess to. Working really puts a crimp in criminal behavior.

"Does that ever work, you asking if pullees know why you stopped them? Better yet, which is the truly stupider behavior: You asking? Or them occasionally spilling their guts?"

I didn't say that. Finally, I just shrugged and said: "I don't have a clue why you pulled me over."

With that, he could tell I was way too smart for him. "You've got a turn signal out. Better get it fixed." And he walked off, looking for a stupider criminal down the road.

Crime doesn't pay. My neck's still got a crick in it.

§

Retirement Monte Carlo

The other day it occurred to me that, since I'm in range of retirement, maybe I should call those folks running the nest where I've been squirreling away money and find out how much I can count on. I did just that; that's what this is all about.

Mind you now, I called them before the stock market melted down a few days ago. That was pretty ominous, that meltdown, and any day now, I expect The Squirrel Nest (that's where my retirement account is) to call me back and say: "You know that bag of pocket gopher feet in your freezer? That one you've been laughingly saving until they go up to a hundred bucks a foot? Well, you'd better count them."
I'd better not only count them, I'd better go after a few more of them. The way the stock market is falling, it won't be long before gopher bounty is worth more than General Motors or IBM.

So, like I said, I called The Squirrels, talked to a Young Squirrel named Lisa. Although it was confusing, I'll try to give it to you the way I heard it.
"Hello, my name is Lisa, and I'm A Squirrel Advisor here at the Squirrel's Nest, how can I help you?"

"Well, Lisa, I'm not getting any younger, and I'd like you to tell me how many nuts I've got saved, and how many I can count on to have when I retire."
"Well, we sure can help you with that, you betcha." (Will we ever forgive Fargo for this 'you betcha' stuff?)

"Good," I replied, "by the way, how does someone get the job of Squirrel Advisor?"

"I have a BS in Nut Marketing, so I get to help folks like you figure out what to do with your nuts. Now, I have some questions: First, do you have any other retirement accounts, like, oh, just for an example, a bag of frozen gopher feet, or, maybe some bags of aluminum pop cans?"

"Yes, I do, how'd you guess?" Boy, these Squirrels are good. I told her that I still had the gopher fund, but that I had to sell the 47 garbage bags of pop cans to fill the gas tank on the truck with which I hauled them to the scrap yard.

"Oh, too bad, but we'll see what the Monte Carlo algorithm says you'll have left to retire on. Just let me input some of your data into it, and it'll give us an infinite range of possible retirement incomes."

"Wait! Isn't Monte Carlo a bunch of casinos where high rollers go to flush their nuts down the drain?"

"Oh, ha ha, sure, that's what everyone thinks, but no, that's not true." Something wasn't true. My built-in bullpuckey detector was ringing like a church bell on Sunday morning.

"You're going to glue a bunch of stick-up notes with different dollar figures to a roulette wheel and spin it, aren't you?"

"Oh, ha ha, giggle. I can tell you've got a great sense of humor. What we really do is define a domain of possible inputs, generate data randomly from that domain, and perform a deterministic computation on the aggregate results, drop poor nuts out of the resulting analytical disorder, and construct probabilistic financial models that in turn either confirm or deny integral multidimensional possible disastrous investment Nut Trees with complicated boundary conditions." (She really did say something a lot like this. I asked her to repeat it so I could write it down. She's obviously a college educated Nut.)

Me: "Ha ha ha, choke, gasp. You're a pretty funny squirrel. Now really, what is it you're going to do about predicting how many nuts I'll have when I retire?"

"I can tell you've got a good sense of humor, so if I tell you what we really do, will you promise not to tell anyone?"

I KNEW IT I KNEW IT! "TELL ME TELL ME ALL."

The nice Nut Marketer said: "We get a bunch of numbers from several callers like you and have a bunch of dice made up for each of you, and we shoot Monte-Carlo-rule craps on coffee break."

"WHAT!?!"

"It's ok. Don't worry. We've got a billion trillion gigabyte computer that cost us about that much in pre-stock-market-collapse dollars, and we've found that, over the volatile past months, just by accident, that the dice work about as well. Of course, all things considered, it will help if you live to be at least a hundred and fifty years old. I have to go, it's coffee break time and the other Nuts have a bunch of new numbers to roll. Do you have any other questions? Hello? Hello?"

§

Singing on Wings of Freedom

Not too long ago one of our friends gave us a pretty little yellow canary, a beautifully miniature bit of living perfection. "Here," they said, "you take her. She won't sing." Perhaps, they speculated, it would be happier at our house, much the same way as an athlete sometimes performs better for another team, or so they may have thought, although I wasn't sure that such a parallel would transfer from man to beast.

After two weeks of languishing silently in its cage, the Old Girl decided to cast open its prison door and let it fly about the house. I thought at the time that perhaps the cat had cast a spell on the Old Girl in order to perk up its diet, but so far, the cat doesn't seem to remotely care.

But the canary, with its new freedom, sings songs that would tire the Philadelphia Symphonic Orchestra. It sings and sings and sings. In the kitchen. In the living room. Not in the cage.

Night before last, rather latish in the evening, I answered the telephone to hear a strange male voice ask me if I had time to talk to an old friend. It was a friend so old that I had to ask him who it was. It was Warren.

Warren and I were very close in high school. He came to our small town in my junior hear wearing a South Carolina accent like a white party dress wears mud. The accent and his brash manner of addressing issues and opinions made life much more interesting. I don't know, or don't remember, much about his non-present father, but he and his older brother and mother had a shirt-tail relative living north of our farm, which is where the two boys stayed. There, they worked (sang?) for their supper, doing chores and farming while going to school. Their mother kept house for someone else, several miles away, which is where she stayed. It wasn't the best; it was the best that could be done.

It worked out, anyway. The older brother now farms around there on his own place, and Warren, who lived at our house a lot and got on great with my parents, finished high school, got married, worked hard, was successful. He moved back to South Carolina after his marriage broke up, and their son, Darrin, went with him.

I hadn't seen Warren since high school, but I kept up with him through my parents, with whom he visited and kept in touch. I felt like it hadn't been that long at all. Like yesterday.

Darrin, who would now be 20 years old, is why he called. Darrin and his girlfriend were among six passengers in a car that missed a stop sign. They were both killed instantly. I knew all that. Dad had told me that in a telephone conversation sometime earlier. Dad also mentioned that I might write him.

I couldn't. I can write about a lot of stuff, but when I tried to write to Warren, knowing even how valuable the letter would be to him, I found myself unable to. Somehow the mixture of all the dread of automobiles that came with now having teenagers myself, and the hypocrisy of suddenly writing someone not because you've been writing to him all along but because his only child had just been killed…somehow it just all turned into painful indecision.

I told him that, and he said he understood. He said that's why he called me. I appreciated that, appreciated it more than I could either understand or say. He intuitively sensed my dilemma, and helped me out with it, at a time when he himself was in one of the most hurtful situations in which a parent can find himself.

He told me all about Darrin. I heard about his gentleness; about his high school wrestling prowess; about the things he said; about the things he was going to do; about how proud old dad was of him; about how old dad always embarrassed him at wrestling meets by being so enthusiastically brash and loud and the typically Warren that I remember. Thank you, Warren, for all that your phone call did for me.

Almost-16 just asked if she could go swimming with, you know, some of the kids. Steve has his driver's license now, you know, dad. Ride along. Limber up wings that for her are free of cares, light of worries. Learn what it feels like to sing.

Sure, I said.

No big deal.

§

Telephones That Crank

The other day, someone was complaining about cell phone service. "Hah!" I replied. "You should have grown up with the first rural party lines." Had they, they might not be quite so upset over what we have now.

You have to understand, though, that growing up in the fifties, the first telephone systems in America— once they reached the rural areas—were regarded with awe bordering on worship. Cranking one and speaking to someone seemed God-like.

One of the first things I remember being told—and believing—was to stay the heck away from that crank phone on the wall when it was storming. At the young age of five or six, the level of the warning that mom gave us was equivalent to a preacher warning the congregation about the devil. "You stay away from that phone, or you'll be sorry!"

Sorry meant there was the potential for a butt warming, something we dreaded not so much because it ever happened, but more because as time went on and it didn't happen, it loomed over us larger than ever. "A good butt warming" was the devil we were afraid of, not the one that lived in the crank phone on the wall.

Then one evening, as we were listening to the Jack Benny show on the radio, two things happened: First, the clap of a close lightning strike nearly deafened us, and two, a blue ball of fire the size of a grapefruit dropped down to the linoleum floor from the telephone and sizzled its way across to the opposite wall, shrinking as it hopped along.

Mom looked up, but barely missed a stitch as she kept sewing yet another patch on someone's pants. The I-told-you-so smirk on her face is mostly what I remember, as we kids scrambled away from the static display rolling across the floor.

I don't remember what dad did. Not much. Since I as the oldest was barely five or six, I'd guess this had been happening regularly enough to both them and the neighbors that neither one of them got too excited. Apparently, this was viewed as yet another demonstration, or proof, of how good life was. That ball of electricity was the frosting on the cake. Better living through electricity.

But, once my brother and I turned into teenagers and discovered girls—in particular, Elaine H.--, lightning wasn't the biggest problem. The biggest problem was Aunt Leah, who operated the switchboard in town. Well, maybe Elaine was the problem. She was a great flirt, and we were both madly in love with her, and for the first time in our lives, that phone on the wall had a reason for being there.

Any time we heard two longs and a short, we knew it was for us. That was our ring. Any other combination, maybe it was for the Harrisons who farmed down the road, or Hendersons, a little further away, or any of the other seven or eight with whom we shared one set of telephone lines. Maybe, it might be the Hendersons calling the Harrisons, and dad might listen in to see if they were getting ready to bale hay. Anybody could listen in to anybody else, as long as they were on our line. There really weren't any secrets. Everybody was equal in income and religion and stuff, so no one, as I remember, got too upset. Often, if someone else picked up and listened, it was one less chore to do to get the word out about the country school Christmas program, and stuff like that.

But Aunt Leah, she was a force to reckon with. Plus, she could listen to everybody.

We'd crank one long ring to get the operator, hoping Aunt Leah wasn't on the switchboard. She almost always was. That was how she knew what was going on all over.

"Yes? What do you boys want!" She'd say, as soon as she heard our voice. Ah, good grief. Aunt Leah's on duty.

"Would you please connect us to Bill Horstman? Please?" Oh how the manners flowed from us when we wanted to get past Aunt Leah.

"And exactly what do you need to talk to Bill about?" Aunt Leah would demand.

"Dad wants to know when he's going to combine oats," we would bluff.

"Your dad never combines oats with Bill; he combines with Johnsons." Like I said, she knew EVERYTHING.

"Is your homework done?" Whoopee. We could bluff her on this one. She wasn't that great at arithmetic.

"Well," we'd reply, saying something like: "Can you help us with this problem, Aunt Leah? If ten horses each have one colt every other year, then who's the president of Guatemala?"

And she'd connect us. For a while. Then she'd break in and say: "That's long enough," and cut us off.

And you thought cell phone service had problems.

§

The Day After Summer

It is the day after. Nearly everyone else has left, and I am sitting alone in the empty haymow of my dad's dad's once-huge red barn. I say once-huge, because it has in some mysterious way shrunk with my growth into adulthood.

At this moment, the haymow and I are alone; it with its emptiness; I with my memories.

The large red banner stapled to the side of the barn says, "Happy 50th Wedding Anniversary, Mom and Dad." Above me in the high dimness of the mow, multicolored crepe-paper streamers weakly protest that it's not quite over, this timely event that took fifty years to get here. They seem to protest that last night's barn dance, complete with hundreds and hundreds of friends, relatives, and neighbors, and a dance band, is still in progress. That it can't be possible that it's over. It took so long to get here, fifty years, it should last longer. Somehow.

Last night, with the evening's start, couples waltzed by on the dance floor with a certain measured attitude of patience in their posture that said the evening is young. No reason to hurry. They paced their twirls carefully as they circled the floor. Around and around.

I thought back, as I sat in the empty mow, to the summer I was seven, and I and my brother couldn't eat Sunday dinner quickly enough to get out into the freshly filled haymow, where each tightly packed bale seemed to stuffed full of summer sun, captured by some magic, evidenced by the warm perfume it emitted. We spent hours and hours building hay bale forts and secret hiding spots. The fresh smell of the new hay was our youth's perfume. Back then, for us, all was summer. And magic. And promise.

Last night, people continued to arrive, drawn to the barn dance to celebrate the anniversary of a victory over our only common enemy—time. As the dance floor began to fill with dancing couples, both the music and the dancers began to chance ever so slightly in measure and note and intensity. It was hardly noticeable, but somehow, this crowd began to realize that, as the night wore on, this, as with all else, could not last forever.

I retreated to the safety of this haymow again as a young man, seeking its comfort from the jolting notice that I still held numbly in my hands. The letter from the draft board said that my friends and neighbors had selected me to report to the nearest United States Army induction center. I spend that next hour of my life in this haymow, hoping to recapture a seven-year-old boy's feeling of protectedness. I sat and considered my options. None contained any magic. My brother had already been drafted. Magic was in short supply, but still I lingered in that haymow, hoping some might appear.

Last night, this haymow-turned-ballroom finally filled up with dancing couples, young and old. Was the band at midnight playing louder? Or did it just seem that way. Were the couples truly dancing with more intensity? Or did it just seem that way. Did everyone sense the rush of time, was that the reason for their feverish dancing? Or did it just seem that way. Seem that way. Seem that way.

I remembered, as I sat alone in my haymow, coming home on leave from the Army. I remember the forced fronts of normalcy that greeted me, at home, at church, in the grocery store. I remember the forced front that I gave them back. See, I said? It's just me.

I remember the two black stars which my parents had placed in their front window, signifying the ultimate contribution to society: their two sons in military service. Then I remember picking my brother up at the airport, his year in Vietnam over. And I remember his eyes. They were no longer the eyes of someone I had grown up with. Here I want to emphasize that if we as humans are ever given the wish to obliterate one memory, I would without hesitation remove what my brother's eyes told me about the end of childhood, about the end of haymows full of summer.

I left for Vietnam three days later, full of the sudden certainty that, for my family, for me, for my friends and neighbors, the haymows of our country were no longer enough to protect us from the future.

Last night, as the evening drew near its end, everyone danced. The children. The adults. The old. The young. An apprehension filled the air. The dancers looked around and saw one another, and saw also that something was ending. Each looked around that haymow full of balloons and confetti and crepe paper and swirling couples and old friends and relatives not seen in too long a time. Each realized then that here was the fire of an old magic, relit in this old haymow on this evening, for them, only. There for them on this evening only.

And oh how they danced, so suddenly filled with this invigorating awareness. The band played as never before. People danced as if they might never get the chance to dance again. The air was heavy with the evening's promise that here, in this haymow full of the lingering smells of summer, time had stopped. And they were young again, and carefree.

Then I was home from Vietnam, and I was hiding once again up in this haymow, searching for my lost summer, examining the look and smell of those freshly mowed bales of alfalfa, hoping that some magic might erase Vietnam. I and my brother got to help dad bale some more of this magical stuff. Helped put some more magic up into that mow, all of us sweating with the heat of summer, reminded that making magic is hard work.

It is the day after. I am sitting alone in my haymow, writing this, trying at the same time to say goodbye and trying to define what exactly it is that I am saying goodbye to. The farm is nearly empty. All the visitors have left.

I see dad coming up the stairs to find something or other. He cannot see me back in the shadows, this magic man who created a life for me and my brother, a life that time turned asunder. But I can see him, and how hard he struggles to get his breath back from his climb up the stairs, this man who has filled this haymow full of summer more than fifty times. I try to remember that to have done that should be a reason for joy. I try. But it is a sweet sadness nonetheless.

The many red and green and blue balloons droop from the ceiling of the haymow, their posture sagging in the breathlessness of their old age. The crepe paper streamers no longer draw tight. They too are now old. The single row of straw bales against the far wall sits lonesome and empty.

My children are in the car outside, shouting for me. They want to go home. I rise unwillingly and make my lingering way to the door, fighting once again a great wave of reluctance to leave this haymow. I have never wanted to leave this haymow.

It is the day after summer.

§

When I Grow Old

When I grow old, don't be surprised if I start to do things differently.

I'll grow my hair out, and my gray mustache. I'll tie what's left of my hair into a ponytail that will astonish people who love me, and puzzle those who don't. When they do look twice, and stare, I will merely reply: "Laissez faire. Let me be. Laissez faire."

For those ill-mannered people who stare, who don't understand the French language, I'll continue to master French words and sayings, partly to exasperate them, and partly because I have a knack for it. To those people who bore me, I will say: "Parlez vous Francais? N'est pa? No? Allez! Allez!'" Which means Get! And don't let the door hit you in the butt on your way out.

The boring people who don't love me will become confused and leave. Those who love me will become too confused to leave. They will whisper to one another: "What are we to do with him?"

No longer will I raise the toilet lid when I grow old. I've been doing it my whole life and I'm tired of it. When you're old, it's a chore to bend over and flip the thing up, so I shan't be able to reach it anyway, should I even want to. And who cares anyway?

I'll have five acres upon which to live, five acres that I will till for as long as I am able, because that is how my ancestors spent their lives--clinging to coveted ground, satisfied from a life made rewarding by harvests from the ground. And when I am no longer able to plow and plant, I will find peace in the time remaining to me, because I know that the ground will continue to honor me with a home, eternally.

I'll have lots of old tractors, two for each acre, because old tractors--with their simplicity and sturdiness--remind me of my youth, when life was simpler, and I was sturdier. I'll keep those tractors cleaned and polished in a heated garage with beaucoup doors in the front, and grande windows to let in the sunlight. Inside, there will be two of every tool, all spotless, one set to use, one to hang on the wall and admire.

When I grow old, you will have to come to my house to see me, because there won't be any telephone. Never again will I have to stop in the middle of lifting the lid, or whatever else I might be savoir fairing, to march off allegro to parlez vous with a tres dumb machine that wants to interrupt you.

When I grow old, I'm going to spend my children's inheritance foolishly, and live in a style to which I am not accustomed. And I'll not save any money for a tomorrow that may or may not come, and may or may not be mine to command when it does come. Before the money is gone, I'll buy fancy ice creams and flying lessons; gaudy old juke boxes full of flashing lights and '50's ballads. I'll have sleek red cars that are close to the ground so it is easy for an old man to fall down into them, but which my children will have to help me out of when I motor splendidly into their yard for a visit.

I'll spend gaily on a lifetime supply of my favorite black licorice, or old tractors at auction, or colored balloons. "C'est la vie," I will say to those who love me and are confused, "C'est la vie."

And finally, when I am gone, those who come after me will say: "Remember when he came to see us in that aeroplane? Or, remember that old jukebox he was always tinkering on? Or, those old tractors? Still confused about it all, nonetheless, they will remember me.

So remember now, and don't be startled when all this starts to happen. Matter of fact, I'm going to practice for when I get old by not liftez-uppez la toilette liddez next time I sashez off to la commodez.

Comprendez vous? Do you understand?

When I grow old, and you come to visit, think before you speak.

And look before you sit.

Don't be surprised.

§

Wood Tick

I sat in church last Sunday and marveled as I usually do at how one's mind tends to ramble past thoughts much more freely there. Is it the austere tones of the interior decorating? The largeness of spirit? The communion with fellow human beings?

Maybe it is telephones that don't jangle, and other earthly tedious demands upon one's mortal soul. Did you ever notice that there are no bills due in the Bible? Well, maybe that one big one.

As I sat there, my mind flowed on past daily concerns, while the pastor linked the Exodus with something that wasn't yet clear, but had some connection with how people are alike but different.

The words of the sermon were a river that carried my thoughts into my relaxed consciousness, one after another, each replacing the previous one. What a nice, relaxing place to focus on the next life.

"I will bring one more plague upon Egypt and the Pharaoh..." went the words of the sermon, which momentarily caught my attention, only to shortly be replaced by the polka dots of the collar worn by the older woman sitting in the pew ahead of me. The dark of the dots against the white background was somehow mesmerizing, as each seemed to change places with the other.

And then one of the dots moved.

"Then go to the Pharaoh and tell him that thunder and hail…"

Outside the window, the sun went under a cloud, but my mind jerked to a halt, as it tried to get back to the dot that had moved. I looked back at the collar. Nothing. "When the rain and hail had ceased, the Pharaoh again sinned…"

The Pharaoh sinned again. The dot moved again. I removed and cleaned my glasses. Such a phenomenon as this could have an easy explanation. I put my glasses back on. Nope. That was no moving polka dot on her collar. It was a nice fat wood tick, and yes, it was on the move.

"Locusts shall cover…" Yes, yes, yes, I thought to myself. The land and a couple of collars, besides.

Let's see, I've been in northern Minnesota long enough to be able to figure out what one should do in this situation. Fortunately, the tick was moving left to right, and not up, so I had a moment to select the proper solution to this dilemma. An old story told by a favorite uncle came briefly to mind. A fellow was asked: "How did you get that black eye?"

It turned out, much to the asker's disbelief, that he had gotten it in church that Sunday, when the rather stout lady in front of him had risen to sing the next hymn with her dress pinched firmly in her rear, um, stoutness. "I knew she wouldn't have liked that," said my uncle, "so I reached forward and pulled it out, at which she blacked my eye."

The next week, the friend met my uncle once again. This time his other eye was black. "I don't suppose that happened in church, did it?" asked his friend.

"Matter of fact, it did," replied my uncle. Once again, they had all stood, and the dress was once again entrapped. The fellow next to me reached over and pulled it loose. "I knew she didn't like that, so I pushed it back in…"

I tried to focus. What to do, what to do. Might I tap this extremely proper lady on the shoulder, and say…what? She was notoriously hard of hearing. I'd have to about holler. She would turn around and demand me to repeat what I had said. What would I say? What was proper? Black eyes aren't any fun.

Moses was smart. What would he do? Moses was parting the Red Sea while the tick was heading for breakfast. I briefly prayed. Nothing came. I tried to get the guy next to me to notice. He thought there was something wrong with my neck.

Right then, the lady felt something, or reached back for a hair tickling her neck, and brushed that tick back toward me, toward…where? I couldn't see it. I examined my front, my lap. It had disappeared.

What was that crawling inside my shirt? Could it get there that quickly? Couldn't be that quick. That must be a psychological itch. Nope. I felt that. That was a wood tick. I hate wood ticks. The sermon was only half over. Moses still had to get to the promised land. He said: "Stand firm. Do not flee…"

I fled.

§

Hardware Store at Christmas Time

I miss my hardware store this time of the year. Christmas keeps creeping up on the local men, closer and closer, as they look nervously about and opt for that bastion of male philosophy that says: if you don't acknowledge that it's there, then it isn't. Really. There is one other belief somewhat similar: maybe, just maybe, it isn't coming this year.

As philosophies that guide males go, these two work just about as well as the rest the ones men use, which don't really work either.

After all, how can it be Christmas? Wasn't it just yesterday that the last bale of third-crop hay went into the shed? (Uh, uh. That was September the third, remember? It did in fact take you until November to unload that last bunch, which you just backed in there and left. Maybe that's what's throwing off your calendar?)

After all, how can it be Christmas? My wife's birthday hasn't happened yet, and that's in the third week of Novem…..oh crap! (Uh, huh. You're in bigger trouble than you thought, aren't you.)

It was always this time of year that guys began trickling into the hardware store, talking about needing some half-inch bolts, but nervously eying the kitchen appliances when they thought no one was looking. Truly, the local hardware store is the only store that the prairie husband has any working familiarity with whatsoever, and it's the first place his Christmas shopping begins.

He's been in my hardware store before. He's been down where the nuts and bolts bins are located—the last time when the grain auger finally refused to run one turn more, and where in heck did that vice-grip pliers that was holding the belt tensioner go to, anyway. Those were good ones, too, really rusty, which meant they usually stuck around. It was the new shiny ones that planted themselves out in the hay field to be found later by a brand new sickle bar on the haybine. Aw, heck. There's my gopher trap, too. Aw no, after blaming everyone including the Russians for stealing that tool, he remembers now using it to set that gopher trap. Aw man.

But that was last summer, like yesterday, and here he is feeling like a fish that's flopped up on the shore. For him, the kitchen appliance aisle is as far from the nuts and bolts as the Mall of America is from the rest of us, but he takes up his determination, realizes he isn't going to get another better chance, and sneaks over there.

He's going to give it a shot, anyway. Once his feet begin to move, he feels better. Surely the answer to all his gift giving is over there. He feels like he's moving into the sun. (We put extra lights over the toasters.) After all, he's got almost an hour before he has to go pick up the kids at school. Compared to putting out a combine fire in the middle of a dry field, or delivering a calf when it's below zero outside, or getting the tractor started when it's twenty below, heck, this isn't anything.

He could pick all his gifts now, maybe, get her a couple of things, after all, more is better, and he's got that birthday thing to compensate for. His breathing quickens, and he visualizes her opening that new toaster oven he's going to get her, and how happy she's going to be with it.

Watch him. He's a refugee from the nuts and bolts, over there where the bathroom scales are shelved, and doesn't she use the one at home a lot, probably got it near worn out, maybe that's a good idea, especially since she always complains about it weighing heavy. He stops. He looks. Only the most expensive one for her. He tucks it under his arm like a football fullback, and turns up the aisle. Wow. Look at all this stuff. Electric can openers, electric grills, deep fryers, this is going to be a little harder than he thought, these are all the things he's been giving her for the last Christmases.

But it ain't over til it's over. He grabs a genuine chrome shower rod, and a frilly pink shower curtain, and it's like he's crossed some invisible barrier. He looks around. It's over. He carries his finds up to the counter, and replies, as he is asked if he wants this wrapped: "Nah, just staple the bag shut and tape a nice bow on it or something."

What's this? This is one guy telling another guy who's the boss at home.

Mostly, back when I had the hardware store, the customer was always right.

Except maybe at Christmas.

§

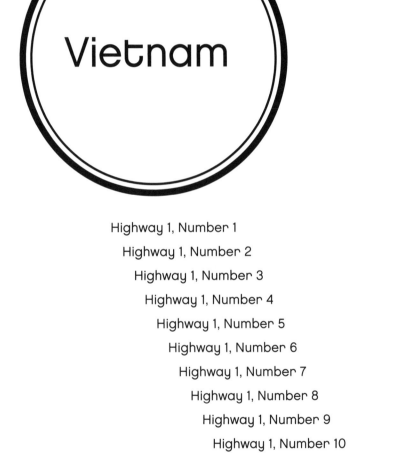

CHAPTER SIX

Vietnam

Although most of these stories are based on fact, time and memory have placed them in a position that I must label "barely true." Let's call them fiction based on fact, or maybe fact based on fiction, and hope for the best. Percentage wise, they're 90 percent true.

Highway 1, Number 1

It was July, 1969, in Vietnam, and Tex and I were headed south on Highway 1 with a deuce-and-a-half truck full of shot-up communications equipment and one M-14 with two clips of ammunition. Riding along with us was of course the fear of the unknown: mines, ambush, friendly fire. The unknown. Ten thousand miles from home. Believe me, there was a lot of unknown, and a lot of fear.

There had been a lot of action up around Quang Tri Combat Base, which was up on the DMZ that divided North and South Vietnam; the LRRP's (pronounced "lurps" for long range recon patrol) were based on one side of us, and the Marines on the other, and they had things stirred up real good. Hence all the equipment in the back of our truck that our bright shining officers had decided was too good to destroy, yet was beyond the point where they thought we should try and fix it. We were taking it south. Dump it on someone else.

I didn't want to leave the base. I'd become rather attached to the false security of a couple of four-foot-diameter culverts with a few layers of sand bags on top. False because nothing stopped the Chi-Com 122-mm rockets that were raining down on us.

Tex and I had earned the honor of this trip through a plan of mine to make some fourth of July fireworks, a plan that backfired.

Each of us on the base was allotted two magazines of ammunition for the M-14. Everything else was locked up. Not locked up on bunker duty, you say? Must have been ammunition to provide for our defense, you say? You'd say wrong. Should you find yourself, and the two soldiers with which you pulled 24-hour bunker duty, under attack, you would crank the field phone and call the sergeant of the guard. The sergeant of the guard would call the officer of the guard. The officer of the guard would call the officer of the day, who was lurking in some underground command bunker somewhere. Exactly where, no one knew. There was a point here in 1969 where fragging officers became a national Vietnam sport, so they were a little reluctant to let it be known exactly where they gathered together. But that's another story.

The command bunker would then crank up their field phone, after having checked with other officers who had the "big picture," a concept that, as we all found out years later, turned out to be nonexistent. No one had the big picture. Vietnam turned into Vietnam because everyone only had their own self-designed, self-promoting, self-sustaining, self-honoring, little picture.

Eventually, with all the field phone glitches and finding all the right officers and the delays involved in all this, the chain of command would eventually trickle back to your bunker. Should Charlie (Viet Cong; VC; Victor Charlie) have been so considerate as to have patiently waited for this process, then you could unlock the machine gun ammo and see if an M-60 that hadn't likely been either fired or maintained within the last 30 days would work. Remember that, latitude-wise, Vietnam is similar to Belize and Honduras in South America--humidity, heat, the whole enchilada. Anything left untended for even a week—including the human body, especially its feet—corroded beyond salvation.

Well, all this is why Vietnam is now the benchmark against which we compare all other military undertakings.

So I scrounged around, being as it was the Fourth of July and someone should take charge of celebrating it, and collected a dozen or so rifle rounds. I removed the bullets, poured out the powder, and built a fuse out of paper and gunpowder. First the fuse, I figured, then the explosive device. I ended up with a paper fuse that looked more like a two-foot-long hot dog.

Tex was in the truck with me—we repaired equipment in trucks that were a lot like small bread trucks. The work area was about ten feet long, with a shallow work bench along each side, and just room to walk down the middle. Anyway, it was well toward a hundred degrees outside when Tex and I locked ourselves in and lit that fuse to see how it burned. If I could get the fuse figured out, then the plan was I'd go looking for some better, more explosive stuff to use the fuse on.

Once lit, the fuse took off like a rocket, zipping around inside that truck like a giant angry firefly. We hit the floor and covered our heads, and when it finally burned itself out, we tumbled out the door choking and coughing amidst the thickest, blackest cloud of gun powder smoke imaginable. It was so thick that it stuck to our uniforms. I looked at Tex. His face was black. Smoke hung out of his pockets.

And there stood Warrant Officer Smith, who had come to deliver some more stuff for me to work on. I looked at him, and in a moment of inspiration, blurted out: "That's the worst radio fire I've ever seen. I think the secondary discriminator is shorted to the high frequency heterodyne raster." Smith couldn't even spell electronics, much less understand any of it. I figured out I was safe.

And he was buying this line of flapdoodle, until a good old southern hillbilly strolled by and said: "Smells lak gunpowder."

Which it did, as any idiot would have known.

Which is why Tex and I were on the road, headed down Highway 1.

Next week: the rest of the trip.

§

Highway 1, Number 2

So there we were, 19-year-old Tex and me, age 25, driving south down Highway 1 in Vietnam, 1969. It was hot, it was humid, and it was scary. As told last week, we had earned this trip as punishment for a 4th of July firecracker attempt of mine that had gone slightly awry.

As punishment goes, this wasn't so bad. Granted, I'd've given anything for a truck that would have gone faster. Those deuce-and-a-halfs—this one loaded up with communications equipment that was shot up beyond our repair—were designed to burn either gasoline or diesel fuel, so they weren't the fastest trucks in the world. A hundred miles an hour wouldn't have been fast enough for me, though.

Tex, though, thought this was a blast. Tex was still bullet proof, like the rest of the 19- and 20-year olds that were sent to Vietnam to make certain the domino effect of communism didn't happen. At 25, though, something had kicked in within me that seemed to remind me every second that there were enough idiots running around just on our side of this military effort to kill me, much less on the enemy's side, too.

I'd already seen the domino effect up close. Once off the airplane that brought me to Vietnam and dropped me and 199 other GIs off in Kamh Rahn Bay, I began to make my way north toward Quang Tri Combat Base, where I would be fixing "Special Electronic Equipment." I was lucky with that. Most of my training comrades went infantry. I was drafted with civilian electronics training, which helped, but what got me this MOS may have been the fact that I had a civilian Secret clearance. Maybe. Maybe I was just plain lucky.

I found an Air America plane loading on the runway, and got on board. Air America humped around the country in DC-3s, twin-prop tail draggers from which all the seats had been removed. This one sat there on the metal runway, its nose up in the air, oil dripping from its engines, a couple of bullet holes in the rear of the fuselage. "Get in here," a loadmaster ordered, and as I and other guys climbed up the steps, we were positioned sitting on the floor, legs out, facing uphill, five wide shoulder-to-shoulder, belted to the floor with four-inch nylon come-along straps ratcheted down tight across our laps.

Lord, it had to be a hundred degrees outside, and inside that tuna can, it felt like double that, the air so stilted and still and full of fear and sweat and strangeness that no one said a word. There wasn't enough breath in us to try. There must have fifty or so of us strapped to the floor, wet through and through with sweat, when the pilot's cap came into view up the steps into the fuselage. He had on a Harley Davidson motorcycle cap, a shiny black silk jacket with Valley of Death stenciled on the back. There was a silver plated revolver showing in a shoulder holster. He carried a jug of water in one hand, and a urine container in the other.

And he looked about 15 years old. So young. By the time I got out of Nam, it occurred to me why pilots were so young: no one with a lick of sense would have flown in the conditions over there. "They're shooting at us around Hue," this kid nonchalantly said to us as he clambered over our laps to get into the cockpit, "so we're flying low and hard." With that, he was gone into the cockpit, and we heard engines begin to crank.

That plane left the ground, caught a strong jungle updraft, and accelerated skyward like a home sick angel, leaving most of us with our stomachs down around our ankles. Out the open side door I could see the tops of trees, and they looked higher than we were. Tropical air currents violently lifted us up, and slammed us down, threw us around. The engine noise through the open side door was loud; the wind screaming by sucked at us. We all slammed left. We all jerked right. The overall effect was something like one might assume a trip to hell might be. Three rows up, close to the front, somebody puked.

That was where I learned about the domino effect. And it wasn't communism they were talking about. Objectively, I thought about what a mess this plane was going to be for someone to clean out. Subjectively, it didn't seem to matter whether we were shot down or hit a tree. I didn't throw up, only because in fact under the pressure of getting to Vietnam, I hadn't eaten in days

Highway 1 on a nice hot day was pretty quiet, compared to that. Tex stuck his hand out the window for some reason to wave at some kids when we eased through a village, and they repaid his kind efforts by stripping his watch and ring. "Kind of keep one eye on your rifle, would you please?" I asked him. He gave me a look. The look said, what? You think I'm stupid?

I grinned at him, and kept driving south.

We're headed down Highway 1.

§

Highway 1, Number 3

This is the third in a series that finds a young GI named Tex and me in July 1969 headed down Highway 1 in South Vietnam with a deuce-and-a-half truck full of shot up communications equipment too classified to scrap, yet beyond repair. As we roll along through not-quite-jungle-but-way-past-forest in this subtropical skinny little country, we pass by small villages. Children race out and shout, in their Vietnamese accents: "GI numbah 10." The ones who have relearned the fact that, in the French-based education they have received, an "A" is a number 10, and in America, it's number 1, so shout. They learn quickly.

The kids hope for American chocolate. (Fat chance. The average temperature several months out of the year here is above the melting point of Hershey's chocolate bars, and they won't eat the tropical chocolate that we get in C-rations. We won't either. Nobody will. Chocolate that won't melt isn't chocolate. It's more like sand mixed with cement.)

Highway 1 is blacktop, and winds down the coastline in a series of s-turns and twists, although the sea is out of sight on the other side of all the growth. Blacktop makes some sense, since it's harder for Charlie to mine. You have to watch the shoulders, though.

We're doing this because I got caught trying to make 4th of July fireworks. I don't want to be on this road. "Don't worry," the first sergeant told me, "we haven't had any reported activity for two weeks now." Or so we were told. And like he would know. That was the thing about Vietnam: even then I suspected nobody told anybody else anything. This was confirmed years later. Nobody, it appeared, knew what anybody else was up to.

As we rolled along the highway, the cursed truck missed and choked and seemed near death at somewhere around 25 mph, and I was terrified it was going to quit out here in the middle on nowhere. Tex had an M-14 with 36 rounds of ammo, two magazines full. That was it.

Wheeled traffic on the road was light; foot traffic almost nonexistent, mostly because even the Ho Chi Minh racing slicks that the Vietnamese wore (pieces of American tires made into sandals) couldn't keep the heat from that blacktop road off their feet. Tex was gawking around as we drove, so I asked him what he'd do if we came under fire.

"I'd hit out into them there brambles, find me a ten-foot-tall marijuana plant, and start eating." Tex was 19. I was 25. Nineteen-year-olds seemed to have different priorities. Common sense probably laid somewhere between him and I, with me taking the ultra-anxiety road, and him the fun one.

Tex had long legs, stood well over six feet. We'd both been in the shower the night before, the shower being a few pieces of corrugated tin nailed up for modesty's sake, and pipe over our heads with holes in it through which river water from a big steel tank flowed. Dirty river mud frequently plugged up the pipe holes, but, regardless of the mud, you could never get clean anyway. One minute after getting out, you were soaked with sweat, which probably explained the "chicken gumbo" growing in our feet, crotch, and arm pits. A very fertile country, Vietnam.

Anyway, it was dark the night before, and Tex had his head lathered up with shampoo pretty fair when a 122-mm ChiCom rocket hit maybe forty yards away, blasting the corrugated tin with gravel that hit like steel ball bearings. In a panic, Tex and I headed for the exit. We both hit the door at the same time, which bounced him—blind with hair shampoo in his eyes-- sideways just enough to stick one of his long legs in a 55-gallon garbage can just outside the shower door. Sirens were howling. The quad-fifties that were parked on our bunker line that week began barking. Men shouted. Flares went up. A Claymore mine down the perimeter went off. All hell was breaking loose, and me and Tex were racing for the protection of a culvert covered in sand bags, him with a barrel on one leg.

And damned if he wasn't winning. A big strong kid, Tex. I figured if the war boiled down to a wrestling match, and Tex went first, we had a chance.

We pulled around one of the sharp curves and saw up ahead four Aussies, whom we could identify by their folded up bush hats. The Australians had a small part of the nightmare that was Vietnam, for political reasons—any reasons—that were beyond me. A small utility vehicle kind of like a four-wheeler with a flat platform on it was tipped over beside the highway, next to a small crater in the shoulder. The men were sharing in the placing of a body bag on a helicopter that was sitting there cranking, ready to take off.

I pulled to a stop. The deuce-and-a-half quit. I cranked the electric starter and prayed. It started again, and backfired. The slick had taken off, and when the pilot heard what sounded like gunfire, he momentarily swiveled his door gunner our way, and then they flew off, leaving us alone once again.

We were ten thousand miles from home. I wondered briefly what everyone back in the world was doing. It was July, so dad had the first crop of hay up, and the corn cultivated twice. Mom's flowers would be in full wondrous color, and she'd be watering the garden.

Tex was hanging out the truck window, waving merrily at the helicopter as it flew off and left us.

I remember feeling really alone as I let out the clutch.

We're headed down Highway 1 in Vietnam. It's 1969.

§

Highway 1, Number 4

It was July of 1969, maybe not the hottest month in Vietnam, at least, not hot enough to keep me and Tex in our army truck off Highway 1, which wound its black-topped serpentine way down the coast, making one mile south for just about every one mile winding sideways through light-to-heavy jungle and the occasional rice paddy.

When it got real hot, the tar road got too soft for truck traffic. They had road restrictions for heat like Minnesota has for frost in the spring. When that happened, the Vietnamese walked somewhere else--they sure didn't walk the shoulders, though, because Charlie planted an assortment of antipersonnel mines in the soft earth there: toe poppers—which clicked when you stepped on them and exploded when you lifted your foot; bouncing bettys—which jumped up into the air and went off somewhere around your gut; and anything else that would explode.

"Whatever you do," my First Sergeant said, "stay on the road." So we were staying on the road, Tex and I, headed south with a deuce-and-a-half truck full of shot up communications equipment.

The truck was running pretty good, after a spell of jerking and dying, although 25 mph was pretty well as fast as it wanted to go. So 25 mph was what we were going when we rounded a curve and found an APC (armored personnel carrier) blocking further progress. A flak-vested GI standing there pointed off to our left at a road that disappeared into the jungle.

"Tex," I said to the guy riding with me as shotgun, him armed with an M-14 and 36 round of ammo, "ask that guy what's up." I pulled up. Tex hung out the window, whooped, slapped the door beneath him and said: "Hey man, how're they hanging?" Tex thought this war was better'n a boy scout jamboree. He failed to comprehend my more serious approach to all this fun.

It turned out that the grunts were sweeping through, hence anything that moved was a fair target, and were sending traffic toward the coast along roads that wound through a couple of villages. He showed us on a map where he wanted us to go; said: "We just run a dozer over into the back of that hamlet, so you can make it, and you can pick up the main detour other side of it."

Perhaps I was just too apprehensive. I shifted down and turned into a trail torn into the jungle. The truck stumbled and missed and started losing power again. Branches grabbed at us.

This truck was probably the same deuce-and-a-half Tex and I'd used to haul a load of garbage out to the landfill a month ago, which the lifers had crazily positioned a mile outside Quang Tri Combat Base. "You can either take that garbage run, or burn shit," said the platoon sergeant, as he was handing out duties. Whoa. No contest. All outhouses on all combat bases sat over 55-gallon barrels. Every day, some lucky guys got to go around, drag those barrels out, stir in fifteen-twenty gallons of diesel fuel, and set them on fire. You had to keep stirring, make sure it was all burned up. Vietnam didn't smell all that good a lot of the time. Neither did the guys doing the burning. We took the garbage run.

So, a month ago, out through the main gate me and Tex went, a truck with no tailgate piled high with all kinds of cans and assorted crap. We made it through Quang Tri village okay, found and turned into the land fill clearing in the jungle, and looked the situation over. I worried about an ambush. Tex didn't worry. He was 19. He was gawking around, soaking in the scene, having a good time.

"Listen, Tex," I said, "it's down hill to the pile there. I'm going to turn around, back up real fast, hit the brakes, slide the load out, and we'll get the hell back inside the base, never have to leave the truck, okay?" We'd be safest that way, I thought.

Tex was bouncing around as I picked up speed backwards down that grade, which was maybe just a little steeper than I'd reckoned on. I was bouncing around. Cans were flying over the hood. Maybe I wouldn't even have any load left by the time I slammed on the brakes.

I slammed down on the brake pedal, the pedal went stiff for a second, and then went all the way to the floor. Brakes were gone. We're careening around inside the cab, gathering velocity backwards. I yelled to Tex: "SOON AS WE HIT HEAD FOR THE JUNGLE!!!" We hit the giant pile of garbage at the bottom of the hill, came to a sudden halt. Tex was out his door and gone in a flash. I couldn't get my door open. I slammed it into whatever was holding it five or six panicky times, and then Tex was there laughing.

I settled down, got my panic under some control, looked out the door. There was a marijuana plant ten feet tall with a trunk like a small tree that kept me from opening my door. It was everywhere over there, and very potent. It kept me in the truck. It kept us soldiers from lots of things, it seems to me now: homesickness, helplessness, the high price of war.

We're on the road south. It's Vietnam, 1969.

§

Highway 1, Number 5

Tex and I are headed south from Quang Tri Combat Base, which is way up on the DMZ in South Vietnam. We're headed for Da Nang with a truck full of shot-up electronics equipment.

It's July, not the hottest season in Vietnam, probably only low 90's, relative humidity hovering somewhere around soup.

.   We had just turned off Highway 1 onto a detour road bulldozed through forest. The growth is impressively heavy, and we drive slowly through it with branches and bushes grabbing at the truck, I'm forebodingly aware of how vulnerable we are, and of how far from The World we are. "Back in The World," that's how we talked about home.

But, after all, from the army's point of view, we are merely one truck and two soldiers, the loss of which won't even raise a blip on anyone's screen. I'm aware of that, too.

Tex isn't. He's leaning out the window grabbing at branches, and though I warn him, it isn't until he has torn his hand open and is bleeding all over everything that he begins to get it. What got him was "wait-a-minute" vines, because once you're in them, you have to literally unhook whatever is hooked, skin or clothes. The thorns have hooks on the ends, like sharp darning needles.

Tex is holding his hand outside the truck, dripping blood, when we come out into a small clearing with a few hooches centered around a small gazebo-like Buddhist temple. The hooches have tin roofs, and I think I recognize my roof from back at the base. It left in a China Sea hurricane that reached inland to us and removed nearly all our roofs last month in a three-day and two-night blow with winds that never dropped under 70 mph, and, as I found out many years later, 55 inches of rain during that week.

I'm only going about ten mph when a small short-haired dog runs out of nowhere in front of me and I feel the thump of my left front tire running over something. An old man sitting cross legged in front of the candles and china figurines before the little temple gets to his feet and slowly comes over just as I stop and get out of the truck.

It was a strange scene: Tex was holding his right hand out to keep the flow of blood away from himself; the Buddhist monk, both of his hands out of sight in his robe; the dog just behind the tire; and me. It was an unreal scene.

I reached into my back pocket and pulled out my old worn wallet, and offered him some American money and a handful of MPC. MPC, military police currency, was monopoly money invented by the U.S. government to control black market and drug trade. It was actually about the size of monopoly money, no less, printed on paper that didn't last too long, which didn't matter because, without warning, we would be notified to exchange our old MPC bills for new, different colored and styled stuff. Anyone who had a whole gob of it had to account for where it came from. And of course no Vietnamese native could exchange any. So they liked dollars.

The monk held both hands up in denial, turned his head and said something to one of the hooches, out of which came an old mama-san, her teeth blackened from chewing the betel leaf, her head in a conical straw hat, who picked up the dog and promptly sat down and began to butcher it for the stew pot.

The monk said something else, and a young daughter-san came out with a couple of GI bandage packs, which I tied on Tex's hand. The monk then turned to me—me with my wallet still in my hand—and held out his hand for my wallet.

I looked at him. I looked at my wallet. Thought to myself: "huh." I slowly handed over my wallet, which he gave to the young black-pajama clad girl who disappeared with it. Then he ushered us over to the third hooch and sat us down, whereupon we were fed some fish and something like potato with very dirty salt. As we were eating—Tex, oblivious to everything, since he was always starving-- the young girl came over and held a wallet out to me, which I took and examined.

I looked over at the half-butchered dog just to make sure that they hadn't turned that one into this dog hair wallet in my hands. I looked inside. Everything was there. The old monk made a gesture that this was much better. He pointed to it and said: "Numbah 10, GI," and smiled proudly. Ten is very good. A ten in France for a grade is like a four-point-oh here. The Vietnamese picked that up from the French.

I had that billfold several years. When it got damp with body sweat, it smelled like wet dog, but with the grain of the hair grabbing backwards at your pocket it was almost impossible for it to slip out.

I bowed to the old monk and grabbed Tex before he ate these folks out of house and home.

We got back on the road again. It's Vietnam, 1969.

"Hey," Tex said, as he turned to me, "do you smell dog?"

§

Highway 1, Number 6

Before I get any older, I'm reliving this trip down Highway 1, in the month of July, 1969. I decided to do it before it's all screwy, instead of just parts of it.

We're driving a deuce-and-a-half truck full of classified secret but shot up electronics equipment, and so far, it isn't even noon, we haven't even gone 10 kilometers of the 90 or so from our home base of Quang Tri, and we've had a couple of mini adventures.

As we roll along through the "mountainous" (north) end of South Vietnam--flat rain forest broken by abrupt large hills--there is no doubt we're not in the U.S. Over on the right, as we roll along, we see intermittent rice paddies, and small hamlets of a dozen or so hooches. On the left, we pass an old man driving two water buffaloes around in a circle on a small platform, knocking rice out of its hull.

Seeing the more agricultural side of Vietnam somehow reassures me that life goes on. The Viet Cong are pounding us regularly now at our base, rockets and mortars which come in a random sort of steady fashion. Sometimes two or three nights will go by and dusk will come quite peacefully. Then all hell will break loose two or three nights in a row. We're continually reminded at daybreak of our puny mortality when we look at the splintered wood and torn corrugated tin that used to be our buildings. We're putting in long grueling evening hours cleaning up the debris, trying at the same time to keep up with the daily workload.

I'm favoring the right side of my right arm and leg a little from three nights ago, when an explosion knocked me out of my canvas cot. It wasn't the explosion itself, it was when I woke up outside on the gravel path leading to the sandbagged culvert where we take cover (hide) during these attacks. The waking up part was alright; unfortunately, I was lying on my right side, running full speed. Instinct got me out the door while still asleep; lack of sight and balance let me fall. I tore up the skin on my arm and leg pretty good, and now, after finding fly eggs in the ragged meat of my forearm, I have to pay better attention to it; otherwise, there'll be maggots in it. Which, maybe, isn't all bad, the natives say. I'm just not sure I'm up to it, hygiene wise.

Someone had duct taped two fragmentation grenades together and pitched them up onto the new major's hooch roof, which was right across the footpath from my bed. The grenades, instead of falling down between his sandbag wall and hooch wall, rolled off the roof and up against my sandbag wall. Frags are pretty impressive, blast wise.

The new major thought so, too, because he had me and a GI named King spend a day and a half welding steel PSP up inside his sleeping area. PSP—portable steel platform—is a sheet of very heavy metal used to make a landing strip on ground like

Vietnam's, ground which is too soft to land on directly. The perforated steel sheets link together, and it's heavier than heck, which the major knew, apparently. King and I sweat like pigs putting that stuff up, and we thought—hoped--maybe the major might expire of heat stroke in the night, trying to sleep in there. That first night after we finished, someone snuck up on his roof and painted a bullseye over his bed. I've still got a picture of it somewhere.

The new major came in about three weeks ago, and next thing you know, on top of getting the crap blown out of us, we're shining jungle boots and standing formation in direct sight of the perimeter, and of the jungle not far outside that. Stupid. One rocket, sixty men gone. Some GI decided this extra grief wasn't necessary, tried to frag the major, and nearly got me.

I took another tack, wrote a fairly detailed accounting of all this, and, before mailing it to my U.S. Senator, stopped and showed it to the C.O. I told him what I was doing, and gave him a copy. He didn't say much. A month later, he called me in and showed me a pile of paper on his desk about six inches thick. The top one was a letter of inquiry from General Westmorland himself. "You've caused me an unbelievable amount of paper work here, Specialist," he said to me. But he said he appreciated me warning him that it was coming. Toward the end of my hitch, he tried his best to get me home for grandpa's funeral. He was tough, but fair. He never minded a fair fight, he told me, one that was face to face.

Me neither. Unfortunately, one thing you could say about Vietnam was, it wasn't a fair fight.

We're on the road, headed south. It's hot, and sticky, but we're headed for the Pass of the Ocean Clouds, north of Da Nang. It's Vietnam, and it's 1969.

§

Highway 1, Number 7

"Let me drive, will you?" Tex asked me as we rolled south on Highway 1 in South Vietnam. It was 1969, and the Tet offensive the year before that had nearly destroyed the town of Quang Tri was barely a bad memory, and, since GI's were rotated through annually, no one was around Quang Tri Combat Base--our base--who had been through it.

Right there, in hindsight, you have one of the biggest reasons Vietnam was such a FUBAR operation. (Fouled up beyond all recognition.) GI's stayed a year; officers six months. Nothing that was learned was passed on; each new generation of officer or enlisted man made the same mistakes, based on the same mistaken impressions and information—impressions and observations which logically enough came from people who also were new.

Tex and I had left the base earlier in the day with a truck full of blown up and broken electronics gear, which we were to deliver to Da Nang. Why, I didn't know. It was junk, full of bullet holes, water, dirt, and crud. CRUD: corrosion, rust, unidentified debris. A lot of the tags on the stuff in the truck behind us was marked with those initials.

"How come you want to drive?" I asked Tex, a big 19-year-old kid who seemed to regard all this as a day trip to a state park. Like all the new 19-year-olds, even the old ones, he was bulletproof. I had turned 25 in 'Nam. I spent the first rocket attack trembling in a dark sandbagged culvert while my heart attempted to pound its way out of my chest. It all seemed pretty clear. That giant whose exploding footsteps walked your way in the dark didn't care where he stepped. It was your turn, then it was your turn. Bad luck, sorry.

It turned out that Tex wanted to say he'd driven down Highway 1 while he was in country, and, since at any speed over 25 this deuce-and-a-half shook you like a dog shakes a rat, I didn't figure he could kill us. I pulled over and we traded places, while a couple of peasants in black silk pajamas in a rice paddy next to us ignored us.

I wasn't totally sure he couldn't kill us. I'd had my folks send me a ten-minute egg timer because you couldn't trust the kid on top of the bunker to stay awake while you tried to catch some Z's down below. Three GI's, each two hours on, four hours off, 24 hour duty. These bunkers were spaced along the circular perimeter of the base, about a hundred meters apart. You looked out at the jungle over triple concertina wire, outside of which was elephant wire—razor tipped wire strung in diamond shapes on stakes, so Charles couldn't run through it, or crawl under it. There were Claymore mines interspersed through the elephant wire.

Nonetheless, a 19-year-old got his throat cut four bunkers north of us. How, no one said. You'd occasionally hear bad stuff that happened; you'd never hear why. Probably went to sleep. Once I got the timer, I'd pass out from exhaustion for ten minutes below, wake up, go up topside, wake up the kid, do it again. You spent a lot of time exhausted. It wasn't only the lack of sleep. It was the constant anxiety, endless oppressive heat and humidity.

We came around a curve and off to the left saw the South China Sea, blue and peaceful. All of a sudden, Tex, who is now driving, turns the truck to the left and we're driving down a sand road headed for the ocean. "What the @#$% are you doing?" I asked him. Army talk. Jungle on the left, jungle on the right. Shit like this got stupid Americans killed.

"Let's just go down and look," he said. You're beginning to see what I mean about anxiety. We pull around some shrubbery growing up on sand pushed up by the ocean, and there's a bunch of army jeeps and a couple of trucks and a bunch of GI's down there, all kind of excited.

It truly was quite a sight for a guy who grew up in Iowa. Out on the ocean, which had about a ten-foot swell going, you'd see small fishing junks with random-firing engines. They'd ride up high on a wave, bang smoke rings a couple of times, then drop down out of sight to reveal a huge U.S. battleship headed the opposite way, so big that it was unaffected by the waves. It rode level steady; the junk rose up and down. If I never see another juxtaposition of contrasting cultures so starkly illustrated, may I be struck blind. All the Vietnamese wanted to do was raise rice and go fish. Maybe all the U.S. was good at was what we were doing, screwing that up for them.

About then, a small Vietnamese boat made its way close enough to shore that some of the soldiers could wade out to it. GI's dragged one of our own out of the boat and brought him to shore, his head hanging. He was in cut-offs, and you could see his dog tags sparkling. The undertow took him out, and he drowned. They worked on him for a while, but it was no good.

A day at the beach for a 19-year-old grunt, maybe. Thought he was safe from leeches and night ambushes and humping around in constant waiting for whatever was going to happen, and he gets dragged under and buys it in the China Sea. Xin loi. Sorry.

I kicked Tex out of the driver's seat, backed the truck the hell out of there, and got underway.

We were both pretty quiet for a while. I've got 39 days to go. Each hour weighs a ton, each day is an eternity, and I can feel the weight of their yet-to-happen-ness dragging me under.

It's July, 1969. We're headed south on Highway 1.

§

Highway 1, Number 8

It wasn't even midmorning, and Tex and I, on our way to Da Nang with a truck full of shot-up and otherwise FUBAR electronic equipment, had already come upon two soldiers who were going home early.

Unfortunately, they were going home in a body bag. Even Tex, who at 19 had up to now shown absolutely no recognizance of his own possible death, seemed to now be newly aware of it. He was seriously examining his rifle over on the passenger side of the vehicle as we went south down Highway 1, traveling from Quang Tri Combat Base up north.

He had been assigned to be my "shotgun," the equivalent of the extra man who used to ride armed as a guard up on top of a stagecoach. I felt a little better that he no longer seemed to regard this as a family trip to Disneyland. I felt a bit more reassured about his attitude.

Then he turned to me and said: "If we see a tiger, stop and let me get a shot off, will you?" Aw, shit. I wished once again that I and the 39 days I had left were back at the base, where I could hide my butt in a bunker, where neither Charley or some reckless 19-year-old with a gun could shoot it off.

On our right, the occasional rice paddy showed up, but for the most part, the northern part of South Vietnam was hilly, and farming was hard. The next stop was Phu Bai, and if one were to examine a map, he would see Dong Ha up below the DMZ, then Quang Tri—our base--, next, Phu Bai, then Hue, then Da Nang.

This end of Vietnam was mostly assigned to the Third Marines, with some support from the army's long range recon soldiers. It was the poor end of South Vietnam, and one marine, upon first seeing Quang Tri Province, had supposedly said: "My gawd! We are fighting to make them take it back, right?"

Anyway, things would calm down a little at the base, then these combat units would sally forth and stir stuff up; next thing you know, Charley is aggravated and raining rockets and mortars down on us.

There were a lot of fire bases established out around Quang Tri, where the big artillery pieces could zero in and help support the ground pounders when they needed it.

At night, up on the 100-foot-tall steel guard tower, you could look out at the night and see tracer rounds and illumination flares around those fire bases. If you looked north, you could see the flashes of 1000-pound bombs that B-52's were dropping. Look south, you saw the same as they carpet bombed the Ashau valley. Some nights you could almost read by the light of the high altitude bombing.

I yawned as we drove along. Last night had been a long one. We'd taken more than a dozen 122's, with the result that our mess hall and some hooches had been leveled. Now we were short two cooks and the kitchen. We'd be eating C-rations for a while.

It's always hard to sleep after a Condition 1 attack. Just to make matters worse, I and the other dozen guys in my hooch were awakened in the early morning hours by the sound of gunfire inside the hooch. Boom! Boom! Boom! How many rounds were fired, I don't know. Several. We were all asleep. It was loud, followed by a long, tense minute with everyone half awake, hollering and waving his rifle around.

It turned out that Jersey, who I'd thought was another 19-year-old. He turned out to have lied about his age to get into the army. He was now barely 18. He'd had enough of the glory of war. Enough heat. Enough lost sleep. Enough lifers. Enough worry. This last rocket attack had pushed him over the edge. So he waited until we were asleep, got out his M-14 .308-caliber rifle, pointed it down at his foot, and tried to give himself a million-dollar wound, which is one that'll get you back to The World. Instead of just one shot, the semiautomatic rifle, after the first round went through his foot, had recoiled, then settled back into his trigger finger. The rifle climbed on him and he'd managed to put at least three more rounds up his leg before dropping it.

It was messy. We got a belt high on his leg to slow down the bleeding and shipped him off to the infirmary. He was going home for sure, but if that leg was going home with him, he would be one lucky guy. It was mangled indescribably. Nobody in and around us slept much more that night.

Tex is aiming his rifle out the window, imagining no doubt a tiger in his sights. I hope he doesn't drop it.

These days and nights, this far from home, I spend a lot of time hoping.

The long blacktop road up ahead seems endless in the wild shimmers it gives off in the subtropical heat. We're headed south on Highway 1. It's July, 1969.

§

Highway 1, Number 9

The sun is reaching that point in the sky where Tex and I, as we're headed down Highway 1 in Vietnam, are being broiled alive inside the olive-drab-colored cab of the army deuce-and-a-half truck that we are driving south. Maybe green is invisible in the jungle we're driving through, but white would have reflected a little of the heat, maybe.

As I think back on it now, most of us were probably dehydrated almost continually. I looked at one of the canteens on the seat beside us, grabbed it and drank a little. It wasn't so bad if you strained it through your teeth and didn't mind the purification junk they dumped in it. I knew the guy who drove a tanker truck up every day to Dong Ha and piped our water out of the river. "Should be good," he said to me, reasoning that that was as far north as the river went. Evidently his geography quit at the DMZ, because North Vietnam was up there, and China on top of that.

The water tasted of everything bad you can think of, so we dumped everything into it we could think of, Kool-aid, orange juice concentrate—you name it. It was still bad. At least they didn't purify it with iodine, which was what the grunts carried with them to treat the water they found. According to my brother, you could tell the FNG's (foolish new guys) because their teeth were stained red from the purification tablets, which everyone else shunned. Their logic at not using it was solid. A good case of dysentery got you out of the jungle.

Next stop, Phu Bai, where another maintenance battalion is located. I've had some minor communication with their electronics guys concerning the Starlite scopes I work on. I think the scopes are the reason I'm not a combat grunt. You need a Secret clearance to work on them, and I had one from civilian life. I also work on mine detectors, most of which work fine when I get them, but the marines get the heeby-jeebies after using them a while, and want a new one. The ones I don't ever see to repair are blown to kingdom come with their operator, I expect.

So I don't blame them for their nervousness. One of the few times I've had to leave the combat base was to head up to Dong Ha with a couple of repaired ones and a couple of new ones to instruct the marines in their use.

"Hey," some two-bar said to me, "you're just in time. Jump into that jeep over there, we're headed out to Firebase Nancy." He seemed to think about something for a while, then said: "We should have you back by nightfall, everything goes well."

When a marine says something like that, it would be like a normal person telling you to be sure your affairs are in order, your end is near.

"But I don't want to go to Firebase Nancy," I felt like telling him. But I didn't. Into the valley of death quietly, honor is everything, die on the battlefield, all that crap. Next thing you know, I'm point on what would barely pass for a deer trail back here in

The World. I've got a metal detector in my hands and well-armed marines behind me. "Everything's probably alright," one of them said to me, adding that there was some activity out here last night and they wanted an expert opinion.

As I waved the metal detector back and forth above the ground, I wanted to tell them that these things don't pick up plastic explosives, but then I wanted to tell them I didn't want to be there at all. It all seemed pretty much like I might as well save my breath. I had a lot of didn't wants these days. So did they.

They didn't seem to be taking all this too seriously, but then, they were marines. Young. Crazy. Young. The young part explains a lot. The rest of it has to be the crazy. I walked around a curve in the trail and down into a dip and the metal detector in my hands went crazy. I froze. The detector showed stuff everywhere. "Get back!" I shouted. "There're mines everywhere!" I stood there frozen, not sure what to do.

I saw the half dozen marines smirking and enjoying themselves. The two-striper took out a knife and dug up three old canteens. "We just wanted to know if these things worked after you fixed them."

When I got my heart rhythm back to normal, I pulled the knobs off the detector I was using, put them in my pocket, and handed the detector to their operator. "Here. I'll keep these knobs. You don't want to get too confused." Which gave them a chance to pick on him. He was an E-2 FNG; I was a Spec 5. Better him than me. All this is humorous in retrospect, but being an FNG and being handed a mine detector was pretty serious, especially when there had been three divisions of NVA in this area only months ago.

The only good thing was I got some C-rats with beans and wieners. Beans and wieners were the good ones.

That was last week.

This is now. This is me and Tex. We're headed down Highway 1. It's July, 1969. I've got 39 days left. They felt like 39 years.

§

Highway 1, Number 10

The long road to Hue from Quang Tri Combat Base in Vietnam back in 1969, when Tex and I headed there in a deuce-and-a-half truck, wasn't measured purely in miles, or klicks, or minutes, or hours.

Instead, as I look back on it now, it seems more to be arranged in scenes and events than in anything else. Obviously, I made it. So did Tex, although to be truthful I have made him several 19-year-olds all rolled up into one, the accumulation of all of their youthful inattentions and general carefree carelessnesses.

Phu Bai Combat Base, which we stopped at to forage up some lunch, and because I had heard that they had air conditioned work trucks and I wanted to see if that was true, turned out to be a disaster. We got some water—which was way better than anything should ever be--but mostly we arrived in the middle of the military equivalent of a volcanic eruption. The entire maintenance battalion was under house arrest.

See, that battalion at Phu Bai had been National Guard over here in the states, located in Boston, Ma., and had been sent intact to Vietnam as a complete unit. Back then, that wasn't done much, and I think after this experiment turned bad, it wasn't done again, not for a long time. My only contact with them so far had been by telephone, and the Boston accent of the guys to whom I spoke seemed to radiate intellect and education. And well it might have, for the average educational level of that unit was between a master's degree and a doctorate, just a bunch of over-educated guys who hadn't wanted to be drafted out of their teaching, medical, and legal careers, so they'd joined the Guard.

Then things changed. Drastically, for them.

The day we drove into their combat base, they had been in-country about six weeks, and they had taken all they could stand. This very morning, they had rebelled. They had had enough morning reveille, enough reconstituted dried eggs for breakfast, enough military chicken shit, illogical orders, enough heat, and enough rocket attacks,--well, anyway, at morning reveille, they proceeded to throw stones at the poor lifer sergeant who had been newly assigned to them. The First Sgt., hearing the ruckus, went out to restore order, and they stoned him also. Their—the rock throwers—thinking was pretty prevalent in Vietnam: Hell! We're in Vietnam—what else can they do to us?

As it turned out, the First Sergeant and the E-7 stayed drunk and hidden for the nearly three weeks that it took for the army to figure all this out and disband the entire unit, shipping it here and there around Vietnam in ones and twos. My maintenance battalion got one of them, and he found out what war really was. After he'd been exposed to some prolonged and truly terrifying rocket and mortar attacks, and twice after sappers got inside our perimeter and flung satchel charges here and there, he began organizing work slowdowns, which he intended to barter for... for what? Had he been realistic, he would have now realized that he and his unit had had it made in Phu Bai. Those bastards had actually had air conditioned work places. Up here on the DMZ we were a little closer to where the action was at that point in the war. Rockets didn't come one at a time, once a week. There wasn't any air conditioned work vans. Our drinking water was truly awful. He had to have realized he'd screwed up.

Did he intend to barter our work for a better life? It was, after all, Vietnam; what better life was there? Less work? When the rockets blew up our sleeping quarters, wouldn't we want to rebuild them rather than sleep in the rain? How about the marines, who needed the radios and searchlights and metal detectors and StarLite scopes we repaired? Should they not get done? And hell! Bottom line—we were not going home, regardless of our behaviors.

He however had his philosophy, and he turned into a major pain in the butt with all his bitching and complaining. We humored him, and ignored him, like the nurses humor the insane at the asylum. He was shortly reassigned, and I never heard of him again.

All this stuff we found out from a soldier with whom we sat after we went through the chow line.

In 1969, morale in Vietnam had hit a new low. Racial strife between the blacks and whites simmered, and had in fact broken out in our mess hall at Quang Tri with group brawls. Drug usage was epidemic. Charlie seemed to know that, after Tet, he was going to win, and he poured on the pressure. We seemed to know it, too, right from General Westmorland on down. Yet, no one was in a position to be the first one to say: "But, the Emperor has no clothes." Instead, each of us—with the exception of the Bostonians—did the best he could do.

It's 1969, we've had a bite to eat, and Tex and I are back in the truck headed south down Highway 1, our canteens full of fresh National Guard water.

It seems like this one-day trip will never end; that we'll never get there.

Thirty-nine days and counting.

§

Highway 1, Number 11

You all have been tagging along on this trip in Vietnam, where Tex and I were stationed back in '69, as we hauled a truck full of shot-up electronics down to Hue.

Some of it was destined to go further, but I think Hue is far enough for now. There have been ten previous accounts of parts of this journey, and for you to have hung in there with me and Tex this far—well, I think Hue is far enough.

It's July, not the hottest month in Vietnam, but not bad. The humidity is so high that our jungle fatigues won't dry if they're washed. So the mama-san whom we pay to do our laundry is washing it in lord-knows-what and hanging it up in a small hooch, where she burns dried water buffalo shit to smoke it dry.

When you sweat, you smell like water buffalo shit.

Tex smelled, which I noticed as we drove on down Highway 1. We were soaked with sweat, what with the green truck roof over us soaking in the hot sun, and the engine in front. One way or another—either sweat when it was hot, or rain in the monsoons—you were always wet. If you weren't careful, weird stuff grew on your feet, crotch, and armpits. The grunts called it "chicken gumbo." It was really gross.

The country around us, up here in the northern end of South Vietnam, was speckled with isolated small rice paddies, whereas down south, much like agriculture here in the States, the fields got bigger. The north end of this country was full of very big hills, one of which, Hamburger Hill, was up around us at Quang Tri. It became famous for the three times the Marines bloodily took it, each time only to give it back to Charley. That way they'd have something to do the next year, I guess, when the new guys and the new officers came in. Hundreds of GI's died in this particular bit of military idiocy.

By now, when we drove through small villages, Tex on his side of the truck watched the children quite warily. A couple of times, we had young men leap into the back of the deuce-and-a-half, hoping for something they could sell on the black market, like cigarettes, or booze.

They'd take one look at the messed up stuff back there—shot up electronics, and jump right back off. "Get ready," I told Tex. "You'll have to crawl back there and throw those guys off if they come back." Mostly I told him that to worry him, which seemed like suitable revenge for the amount these 19-year-olds worried me. And Tex, who was big, could have thrown them off, but he just kind of eyed me, knowing that if they wanted that junk back there, what with most of them having the technical level of third-graders, they could well have it. He didn't care. He was happy riding along. No worries.

As we turned the curve into Hue, I saw the instant mixture of old world charm and architecture and at the same time, the bombed out rubble, too. There'd be a re-markable old citadel—what we'd call a kind of religious fort—and next to it, the rubble of brick and mortar from a thousand-pound American bomb, dropped back during Tet several months ago.

Most wonderful of all was the tall brick wall that encompassed the old part of Hue, with vines and flowers growing out of it. Once we crossed the Perfume River, it felt like a sight-seeing tour, except for the exploded buildings.

Up ahead, the South Vietnamese Army had a road block going for vehicles. All the other stream of foot traffic went right on through, the peasants in their conical rice straw hats, the promenading young girls arm-in-arm in their white outfits and parasols, the monks in their long robes, farmers carrying tied-up pigs for market, bicycles and bicycle taxis and small Honda motorcycles—a veritable sea of people flowing into Hue.

One of the Vietnamese soldiers pulled us over and spouted Vietnamese at me, waving his rifle at me and at the back of the truck. Then there were two of them. Then three. They jumped up on the back of the truck and began throwing stuff around back there. We got out.

Tex looked at me and said: "What the hell's this about?" Like I knew. I knew about three words in Vietnamese, none complimentary. I could swear and say I was sorry, that was it.

"Well, I told them you were from Texas, and they just went crazy," I said to Tex, in an attempt at humor that went south almost immediately as two of the Arvins (Army of Vietnam) backed us up against the truck with their 16's in our face. I found out later that they'd lost a slug of guys the night before in an ambush when the U.S. Air Force didn't respond to their request for air support, and they were now really upset with us. "Blame Nixon," I would have said to them.

Just when things really looked tense, two young teenage Vietnamese boys rid-ing on a small Honda motorcycle went through, and in the process of waving and flirt-ing with all the young girls promenading along the side of the road, lost control of their bike and veered off the road into triple high concertina wire.

Concertina wire has double razor blades every six inches. These boys were about to pay an awful price for their youthful lack of attention. The Vietnamese soldiers immediately left us and ran to help, although, lacking leather gloves and heavy wire cutters, I don't know what they thought they could do.

Tex and I jumped into the truck and sped away. I have to believe those two kids bled to death in that wire. I wanted to think I felt bad about that, and wondered where and when I had lost all empathy for those people. I wanted to go home.

It's Vietnam, July, 1969. We've been headed south on Highway 1, and I've got 39 days left.

§

Burning Prayer Paper

From Quang Tri Combat Base we came down to Phu Bai, me and Tex, with a deuce-and-a-half truck full of shot-up electronics. It was July. You haven't seen hot until you've seen July in Viet Nam. You wore the heat and humidity the way you'd wear a giant C-clamp screwed to your chest, one you knew would squeeze you, at that time, for 228 more days. The heat smothered you; the days left ahead of you dragged you down.

Some of those days were just bound to be longer than some of the others. Today was going to come out pretty okay, because we'd safely made it here. We'd pulled out of Quang Tri Combat Base in the near-dawn haze, real early. It was so early and so quiet as we slipped through Quang Tri City that you could almost forget what the night before had been like, with its sirens and 122s exploding and us running around like rats in a sandbag-walled trap. Charley was going to try and blow you into little pieces that could be sent home in a bag.

On real bad nights Charley came through the concertina wire, laid bamboo poles on it to hold it down while he slipped through.

Charley. That came from Viet Communist, then Viet Cong, then V.C., then Victor Charley. Really, from Charley's twisted point of view, he didn't want to kill you, just wound you real good, which would cause a lot of disruption that kept two or three more GIs busy hauling your ass out, too busy to shoot back.

You wore two dog tags for a reason. If you bought it, they'd stick one in your mouth and tie one to your boot, either or. The Army studied death the way a third-grader studied cursive, real focused in their study, and odds were, you'd have either a head or a foot left to tag.

Combat searchlights, Prick 25 back-pack radios, hand-held mine detectors, and other miscellaneous stuff rattled around back there in the open bed of that truck. It's how many years and nightmares later that it still rattles around in my head, and if I didn't know the exact details of what happened to each of those individual pieces of equipment, the various bullet holes and shrapnel gouges in them told enough of the story so you didn't want to know the rest of it.

At that point in time, I knew enough already. One thing about Vietnam in 1969, there was plenty of story to go around, especially up north where we were. Maybe Saigon with its Dairy Queens and McBurger joints was considered bullet proof, but Quang Tri and Dong Ha, with the Marines still bloody a few klicks out at the Rock Pile and Camp Carroll, and 19-year-old GIs just south of us hanging on to Firebase Betty against the NVA (North Vietnamese Army), in weather that kept air support from flying in to even haul out the wounded and worse. We were pretty busy, ducking and praying and trying to fix this stuff for the warriors.

But we couldn't fix it all, which was why we were trucking it down to Phu Bai. "Okay," our Chief Warrant Officer said yesterday, "who's going to drive the equipment evac down tomorrow?" Exactly how he got in charge of our electronics squad is something I still haven't figured out. He didn't know a voltmeter from his backside. If you need one more reason to explain why Vietnam was so screwed up, you could start with promoting people like him.

Nobody was clamoring for the truck job. Highway One, which wound its way down country, wasn't exactly a pleasure drive at that point in time. Yeah, the holes blown in it from the Tet offensive last year had been repaired, but current thinking was don't send a convoy, that's just more targets. Let's just send 'em down one truck at a time. Less paperwork that way, you lose one at a time.

He looked at me, said "Take Tex with you." And that was that. Tex and me and two rifles and two magazines of ammo were in it now, that was for sure. Tex thought it was going to be fun. At least he wouldn't be trying to pet Vietnamese kids on the head as we eased through villages. They'd stolen his watch last time he tried it.

We pulled in through the gates of Phu Bai Combat Base, and saw half a dozen double-blade Chinook helicopters staged up to haul a bunch of 1st Cav GIs and tiger-stripe garbed ARVNs (Pronounced "arvin,"Army, Republic of Viet Nam, our side) out into the boonies on some FUBARed attempt to win the war again. They all milled around, waiting to get started, stooped over with fear and battle packs and all the ammo they could carry.

That was when I saw the Vietnamese soldiers burning small pieces of paper, holding them up into the air like little candles.

I asked later what they were doing. It turns out that the Vietnamese thought that their ancestors would answer their prayers if they wrote them on paper and burned them; that their ancestors could read the smoke and keep them alive.

From what I heard, what with them avoiding battle every chance they got, they didn't hold a hundred percent faith in those prayers.

I didn't blame them.

With the hindsight of years gone by, it is now clear to me that prayers written on burning paper had just as much chance of success as we did.

§

The Wrist Rocket

I pulled back on the wrist rocket slingshot, and let go into the tall grass behind the bunker line in Vietnam with about a quarter ounce of lead solder. In the darkness of night, I heard the ripping sound of the more or less round ball as it tore through the bamboo grass. I immediately picked up the starlight scope to see if my shot had found its mark.

It hadn't. I loaded another round and aimed at the last place I had seen in the scope the shimmering outline of a human crawling up behind me, maybe two house lengths away. It was hot. Sticky jungle humid, and miserable. I let the second round go, and checked again with the night scope.

Again I had missed. I saw through the scope that the person I was shooting at was frozen motionless, trying to figure out what that sound was. So I was missing pretty close, judging from the reaction. I readied another round.

OK, you've figured out by now that this isn't just another hunting story. In fact, it was 1969, I was pulling 24-hour bunker duty at Quang Tri Combat Base, about 8 klicks south of the DMZ, and it was about midnight. In other words, dark. I was on top of what really looked more like a child's fort than anything else. It was a bunker made out of sandbags, like everything else in my world there, with a three-foot wall around the top, where one might expect Charley to come calling, should he be able to get through the concertina wire, the elephant wire, and the Claymore mines that were woven into the entire formation.

I at that point didn't care much about what was going on in the jungle out front; I was more interested in Sgt. Rust, a lifer whose sole goal seemed to be to catch someone sleeping on bunker duty, steal his rifle, and report this to the officer of the guard. Having done so, he would apparently feel that his efforts toward the war were achieved.

He was a jerk, an uneducated, ignorant lifer, a lot like most of the noncommissioned officers that the army was full of during that time. They'd feel good to put in 20 and get out an E-7. They'd be lucky to get out an E-6. You may not know much about army rank, but I'll tell you, neither of those life goals set the mark very high. These were the leaders upon whom we bet our lives, and I found out very quickly that getting out of Vietnam alive depended upon figuring out how these guys were most likely to get you killed and avoid it.

I was at the moment enjoying avoiding Sgt. Rust. See, the way bunker duty worked was three soldiers looked at a roster, saw their names up there, and reported for duty at 5:00 pm. During that time, you were up on top of the bunker two hours, then off for four. We ate the old world war 2 C-rations that we were issued, and only left the bunker to defecate or urinate, which we did in that tall grass behind us.

During the four hours you were off, you depended upon the guy on top to stay awake, the sum result of which kept you from getting your throat cut like happened to the soldier three bunkers down from the one I was on a few nights previously.

No, that wasn't Sgt. Rust. They found the concertina wire cut, along with the kid's throat, and a satchel charge that hadn't gone off behind the bunker that housed the officer of the guard. Of course, when the alarm was sounded in the middle of the night, suddenly everyone is trigger happy and very excited, and you're just as liable to get yourself shot as you are to shoot the enemy. It's not a good situation.

One of the pieces of equipment that I, due to a top secret civilian clearance, was assigned to work on was the starlight scope, and in the process, I had assembled my own. A major no-no, should I get caught with it.

I let another slingshot round go into the grass, loaded another one quick as I could, and let that one rip too. I grabbed the scope and checked out Sgt. Rust. Once again, he was confused, looking around. Boy, if he only knew I had this scope, he'd have busted me back to LBJ in a heartbeat. Lon Bien jail. Bad place.

I hit him in the tin pot with the next shot, and he stood up and took off running. I later heard that he was heard to say as he was drinking in the NCO hootch that he'd been hit by a spent round.

I wrote the folks for some real steel balls for the slingshot. I figured I'd at least have something to defend myself with, if Charley came through.

All our ammunition was locked up.

It's hard to win a land war in SE Asia when the ammo is locked up.

§

CHAPTER SEVEN

The Tornado

I wrote this short story while still back in college, after I got back from Vietnam. This is a work of fiction. Any resemblance to persons or places is accidental, but there is no doubt that parts and pieces of it came from my life. I didn't write any more like it. They weren't any fun, frankly.

Out behind the farmhouse in which I grew up, planted by my great grandfather as protection against the bite of bitter northwest Iowa winter winds, stood the grove. It was large enough to be, and felt like to me, a little world all its own. It had rabbits and pheasants to hunt, and places for them to hide in the old abandoned horse machinery rusting peacefully away there, like a history lesson of our family. It had wood to buzz saw into firewood. It had box elder and elm and green maple trees that grew close enough together that you could climb up into one and leap to the others from branch to branch. In a way that is both easy to feel and yet hard to describe, I grew up in that leaf-sheltered world, its double center rows of smooth limbs with their fingers laced overhead like a roof against not only hot summer days when the air crackled with humidity, but against anything bad from the rest of the world .

My younger brother Matt and our cousin Robert Michael and I learned the things out there in the grove that weren't included in any school curriculum. Maybe, looking back, we learned things you don't need to know. Or don't want to. Maybe we learned too much.

I guess Robert Michael must have really hated his name, because one day—I remember we were building straw-bale forts up under the laminated arched rafters of the haymow's ceiling—he told us he had decided to change it. Since he was the most creative and proactive of the three of us when it came to play, we agreed with him when he decided Slade suited him better. It was just a name, at a time when each farm morning brought arms that climbed trees higher, legs ran faster, and minds seemed to find no end of new variations of play to act out. Just a name.

But Matt and I would never have come up with something like that. We liked our names. Subconsciously, looking back, I knew even back then that Robert Michael was somehow different. That he somehow didn't like his name. It would, however, have never occurred to either of us that maybe he didn't like himself. Or even that he just visited us, but grew up in another world that was somehow different from ours. Anyway, he changed a lot through those last days of adolescent play.

But the grove never changed. It went along with the seasons, sure, but summer sun or winter snow—those hindered us at our play not in the slightest. The games we played out there changed. We changed. The grove didn't.

We had a small shack of sorts out there, just a bunch of old barn boards nailed against some conveniently located trees, with some sort of roof, maybe old corrugated tin, or something. I can't remember what the roof might have been made of. Not much, most likely.

Slade came up with a pack of cigarettes during one of his summer visits, and I remember how sick Matt and I got, smoking them inside our cramped, dirt-floored shack. How wretchedly crappy I felt, like I'd been spun around in a circle too long, a circle led by Robert Michael, as usual.

L.S.M.F.T. I remember sickly seeing that written on that pack of cigarettes—"cigs" we called them, like abbreviating them made us cooler—where they lay crumpled up on the dirt floor. Even today, the smell of a Lucky Strike reminds me that Lucky Strike Means Fine Tobacco. That smell will come out of a crowd and punch me right between the eyes, right where you get dizzy.

That's one picture I have, one that is still left. Slade with a snow-white Lucky hanging crookedly from the corner of his mouth, his head tipped expertly to one side to allow the smoke to miss his eyes, all while he described Molotov cocktails and how they were made and how they were best used. While he drew in the dirt floor with one hand, his other hand idly picked a flake of brown tobacco from his lip. Neither Matt nor I could even talk and keep the cig in our mouth, and, rather than reveal our weakness, mostly let Slade have the floor.

With an empty Orange Crush pop bottle and piece of old rag, he said, "The only tricky part is getting enough gasoline in the bottle so the rag gets wet enough to burn, but not so wet it drips gas on your arm, before you throw it at the tank." The cig bounced jauntily up and down in his lips, denying gravity—daring gravity—to pull it from those lips, where it so naturally belonged. My brother and I noticed stuff like that about Cousin Robert Michael. Life held few rules for him.

And so we discussed and acted out the best ways to disable an armored tank, or approach a machine gun bunker, or throw a grenade. These war games were the last we played out in the grove. Before them had come cops and robbers, fed by Cousin Robert Michael's seemingly endless and intimate knowledge of Al Capone and Babyface Nelson and countless others. Before cops and robbers had come cowboys and Indians, about which he also knew everything necessary to properly act out our scenarios.

But the war games? They came with our maturing ability to manipulate components of that game that existed around us on the farm, namely, fire and guns. Fire from gasoline; guns from the Daisy BB rifles that every farm boy owned by natural right.

We swiped the gas from dad's tractor barrel, and constructed numerous Molotov cocktails, and hurled them at the old machinery in the grove, which had become enemy tanks, and large boulders sticking out of the ground in the corn fields that surrounded the entire farmstead, which had become enemy bunkers. We stalked, and hurled, and talked about burning enemy soldiers.

Cousin Robert Michael showed us how to wire shotgun shells to the ends of the barrels of our BB guns, so the BB would set off the shell, with lots of smoke and noise. And danger, I guess, which seemed to be what we were after.

These war games came last, and were the end of our childhood games. Cousin Robert Michael had been inspirational at cowboys chasing Indians, and he had brought innovative twists that Matt and I could never have come up with at cops and robbers—but he was supernatural with war and strategy and lines of defense and attack teams and army lingo. Sometimes, he was too much for us to handle. He really got into it, kind of forgot who he was, like.

And that's the second thing I remember, him getting lost in these games. With the tree-filtered summer sunlight casting wiggling ripples on the grove's floor, I can see both Robert Michael and my brother Matt, from where I am trying to arm my BB gun with another shotgun shell. My attention is focused mainly on what I am trying to do, but I look up enough to see Matt from my hiding spot, see him crawling carefully backwards away from the protection of a broken grain drill. I also notice Robert Michael's BB gun barrel jutting from his fencepost bunker, never moving, pointed like a metallic blue finger at a jumbled pile of boards over to Matt's left. Somehow, he knew, probably even before Matt did, just where Matt was going to deploy, just like he knew that no Lucky Strike existed that dared fall unbidden from his lips.

And I only believed after the fact that Robert Michael wouldn't follow the rule of making sure BBs were shot only at a part of the body covered with clothing. So I watched, and wound wire on my shotgun shell, and felt lazy during a moment of sun shining on my hiding space. But I remember Robert Michael's gun barrel never wavering or changing aim, even though I knew he couldn't see Matt move through the tall weeds and pieces of junk between them. But he knew just where Matt's head would come up, and he waited for his shot.

Robert Michael's BB hit Matt in the left lens of his glasses. It made a sudden clinking noise like a tea spoon dropping into an empty coffee cup, and my first thought was to believe that the BB had missed and hit a piece of metal machinery. But that was replaced by the reality of the red blood running down Matt's cheek, and his cries of pain as he grabbed at his eye and rocked back and forth.

Robert Michael never visited again. Maybe he was ashamed of what he had done, but that's doubtful. More like he, like us, knew the games were over. It was his last shot.

My next visit to the grove was a long, long time later, with my mother. I was on leave after army basic training; cousin Robert Michael was in Fort Benning, in the army's noncommissioned officer school, where he had gone after advanced infantry training, and Matt had just been assigned to the 196th Infantry Battalion in Vietnam, somewhere in and around Chu Lai, but he couldn't tell us exactly where in his first letter from there, in case the letter was intercepted by the enemy. His eye had healed up over the years since he had been shot, but the doctors said it would never be as good as the other one. It was good enough, the army said.

In a letter to me, Matt said he was going to see if he could get a transfer to Robert Michael's unit, when he got in-country. Slade, he said and I had to agree, was going to be a natural at running around in the jungle looking for Charley. I—God help me, we were still so innocently playing at games that had not until now involved our lives—I wrote back and light-heartedly said that I too would try for assignment with them both. Wouldn't that be a kick.

The army agreed that all three of us were above average in war skills, evidently. They said our tests warranted sending all three of us to NCO school. I went to the farm while I waited for orders for advanced infantry training. It was autumn. The leaves of the trees in the grove with their reds and golds were like fire up there in the sky.

I went to the grove with mom that fall day, just to walk and talk under the dappled canopy of those trees, where the rural quiet was broken only by the background drone of insects and the faraway sounds of a neighbor's tractor, picking corn. Mom was really strung out over the whole Vietnam war and its claim on her two sons. I thought maybe a visit to the calm of the grove would help—dad suggested it, I guess.

As she talked about the new medicine that the young doctor in town had prescribed for her to help her sleep, I remember wondering when her hair had gotten so grey, and when her hands, with which she scratched nervously at her bare forearms, had become so restless and out of control. She began to cry as she said, "I don't know what's wrong with me. I never would've let stuff like this bother me before."

After another spasm of sobbing, she said, "You boys know how proud of you we are…" And fresh tears tore away the rest of what she wanted to say. Or the years between then and now took it away. I wasn't concentrating at my best during that time. None of us were. Vietnam seemed to be all any of us thought about, all the television showed every night. All politicians talked about. It was everywhere.

It's three years and three months later. Dad and I just now came back from the grove. We're sitting at the kitchen table. I'm sitting where I sat growing up. My initials are still visible on the table leg to my right, right where I carved them with my first jackknife. There's a cup of coffee steaming on the worn and scratched table top in front of me. This home—this house in which I grew up—feels uneasily familiar and faintly strange to me, all at once, like I both do and don't belong here anymore. Dad and I are learning to talk about things besides farm auctions and tractors and the neighbors, when I come to visit. We're trying, anyway.

Mom killed herself with a drug overdose, about two weeks after two army officers drove into the yard in a dark green sedan with the news that Matt had been killed while trying to rescue a downed pilot up in the hills close to Cambodia.

Maybe if I had been with him, to help him see, my two good eyes would have….I don't know….have helped. Somehow. I don't know. Maybe I could have stopped Cousin Robert Michael that day in the grove, way back when we were kids, before he pulled the trigger on Matt's eye. Then maybe Matt would still be alive. I think about it a lot. I wish I would have been there for Matt the first time, in the grove. I should have been there, the second time. It feels like I haven't been anywhere I should have been.

These days I know more about emotional illnesses and stuff about the kind of emotional upset that accompanies menopause in older women, but I didn't know much then, when Mom and I went to the grove. Mom had said she'd be all right, don't worry about her. Maybe I could have gotten her to a psychologist, or something.

Out in the grove, that's where dad said he found her. He said he thought she'd just fallen asleep, the way she was curled up there in the roofless remains of our old childhood shack. That's the most he's ever said about that.

Cousin Robert Michael is still up in Canada somewhere; we don't hear anything from him. He went AWOL when his orders for Nam came. Dad and I talk about his doing that, because it's the safest thing we can really talk about. Dad says Robert Michael's parents never gave him the opportunity to grow up, the room to grow up. I think he might be better off for not having grown up. He's alive.

I can see the grove from where I sit, through the two white-curtained windows in the kitchen, out past the faded red barn, through the steam rising from my coffee. Part of me is here, and part of me is still back there, with all the hell of the momentary violence that broke down on us at nightfall, mortar rounds falling out of the dark like rain, the popcorn sound of intense rifle fire, our jets laying napalm just about in our laps. Every time it happened, I would believe that if I could just get back home to the grove, everything would be all right again. Everything would go back to the way it was. Then daylight would come again to the jungle, and with each new dawn I would choose between staying under the triple-canopied jungle of Vietnam, and a hope-starved existence, or going home to the grove, the one with elm and maple trees, and no brother, and no mother.

I was into my third hitch over there when the war ended, and my choice was made for me. I had to go home. That was three months ago.

Like I said, Dad and I were just out in the grove. It looks like it hurts, all torn up and twisted every which way, my trees fallen down and jumbled up like a bad throw of pick-up sticks.

Nothing out there looks the same. Dad said a tornado went through while I was in Vietnam, and tore everything up.

I guess it did.

§

Direct Order Form

The Prairie Spy: Who Shot the Dryer? And Other Stories From the Home Front

Fax orders: 218-385-3708

Postal Orders: Trellis Publishing, Inc.

P.O. Box 280

New York Mills, MN 56567

Bill and Ship to:

Company Name: _____

Contact Person: _____

Address: _____

City _____ State_____ Zip _____

Daytime Telephone (_____) _____ E-mail_____

Ordering Information

	Retail	Quantity	Price	Total
A Prairie Spy	$12.95	_____	_____	_____

Quantity	Discount	Price
3-4	20%	
5-24	40%	
25 or more	50%	

Shipping:	Order amount	Shipping and Handling	
	$20 and under	$4.00	
	$20.01 - $40	$6.00	
	$40.01 - $70	$8.00	
	$70.01 - $160	$10.00	
	Over $160	6 % of order	_____

Minnesota residents add 6.5 % tax   _____

Type of Payment

Check enclosed, payable to: *Trellis Publishing, Inc.*

Credit card: _____Visa _____Mastercard ____American Express

Card number: _____

Name on the card: _____ Expiration Date: _____

Signature: _____